SECRET
ROCKFORD

EDITED

By

MICHAEL KLEEN

Secret Rockford

ISBN-13: 978-1530761807

Published by Digital Ninjas Media, Inc.

To order copies of this book contact:

Digital Ninjas Media, Inc.
Rockton, Illinois
www.digitalninjasmedia.com
www.heathnwanda.com

Printed in the United States of America.

For the truth seekers.

"For everyone who does wicked things hates the light and does not come to the light, lest his works should be exposed. But whoever does what is true comes to the light, so that it may be clearly seen that his works have been carried out in God." - John 3:20-21

"Toad Hall" by Jami Beck

CONTENTS

FORWARD

JIM PHELPS

Secret Rockford: The truth you will never know.

Rockford has more scorpions under its rocks than the Mojave Desert. This book of independent authors highlights those stories—from good to bad and downright nasty—that none of the powers that be want you to know. For knowledge, the saying goes, is power, and the Powerful want you to be powerless.

By reading these stories, you will kick over just a few of the thousand secrets in Rockford that will never see the light of day, and maybe kill a few scorpions in the process.

Take, for instance, the story of how the effort to protect a Coca-Cola ghost sign on the former site of Lillian's Clothing Store on the 200 block of 7th Street resulted in a gerrymandered shopstead building project.

See, in the mid-1990s, the powers that were (be) decided to rebuild a gap in the streetscape with development money and create city two shopsteads. However, the most important aspect of the project was a 1903 ghost sign that some of the 7th Street Association members thought was an interesting part of the social and cultural heritage of 7th Street. So, they had these two city shopsteads built around this sign. They were absolutely certain that the good people of Coca-Cola would be happy to repaint that sign for them.

Did the 7th Street Association ask, on the front end of the project, if the Coca-Cola Company would cover the estimated $50,000 for the reworked art sign? Naw... that would be what normal folk with common sense and average intelligence would do. In typical Rockford elitist, top-down, authoritarian leadership fashion, that bit of common sense and good project management eluded this group. What they proposed instead was a gated barrier to protect their new, virgin building from all the undesirables of 7th Street, as well as a courtyard and alley where lights would point upward onto the Coke ghost sign, which was soon to be restored to its 1903 glory, they assumed, by the Coca-Cola Company!

Laughably, only after the project was completed did the 7th Street Association approach the Coca-Cola Company to kick in their fair share of the cost to repaint the sign. The 7th Street Association received nothing. Zero. Not a single penny. One could easily imagine the Coca-Cola executives scratching their heads after reading such a strange request.

Why, cried the 7th Street Association, would you not want to protect part of our cultural inheritance here on 7th Street, mighty CokeCorp? Because, dummies, replied the mighty CokeCorp, that sign was first painted when we used to have cocaine in Coca-Cola! Why would we want to highlight that part of our corporation's heritage?

Secret Rockford.

There is more to the story here than you will ever see in print because to tell you the truth, the whole truth, would be more damaging than you think, and the powerful can't have that. I assure you, however, we can have that, and we will be a better community for killing a few scorpions in the process of overturning those rocks.

> – Jim Phelps, observer of the old Coke ghost
> sign and other Rockford stupidities.

PREFACE

MICHAEL KLEEN

In the past several years, a lot of angry ink has been spilled over Rockford's embarrassing inclusion in a series of negative lists. In May 2011, 24/7 Wall St. listed Rockford as the 9th most dangerous city in the United States, while later that fall, *Forbes Magazine* listed Rockford as the 10th most dangerous. In 2011, *Forbes Magazine* also listed Rockford as the 9th "most miserable city" in the country. In 2013, Rockford climbed to third place on that list, while RealtyTrac claimed Rockford also had the 3rd slowest real estate market recovery in the country. That same year, NeighborhoodScout.com labeled a large area of south central Rockford as the 14th most dangerous neighborhood in the country. In 2012, Rockfordians ate their way to 4th on Gallup-Healthways Well-Being Index of most overweight metro areas in the United States, with an obesity rate of 35.5 percent.

Comedy Central's *The Daily Show with Jon Stewart* even got into the act. In a March 2011 segment that lampooned 13 Democratic state senators from Wisconsin who fled to Rockford during a fight over collective bargaining, Daily Show reporter John Oliver visited our city to interview Wisconsin State Senator Jon Erpenbach. He even spoke with David Hale, leader of the Rockford Tea Party, whose ambush-style footage of several Wisconsin senators at the Clock Tower Resort and Conference Center made national headlines. As Oliver's car drove down East State Street past rows of fast food restaurant chains, he described the scenery as "mile after mile of unforgiving terrain, devoid of any sign of humanity."

Rockfordians responded to this negative publicity with a diverse mixture of stoicism, humor, and righteous indignation. While the Rockford Area Convention & Visitors Bureau ran a low budget ad campaign called "Misery Loves Company," local videographer Pablo Korona created *Our City, Our Story. Our City, Our Story* was a series of videos intended to "tell the stories that if you're from Rockford, they make you proud to be. The stories that if you've never been to Rockford, they make you want to come here." Similarly, Exhilarate Rockford invited the public to share on its website what they love most about their city in 170 characters or less.

Websites like RkfdNews, on the other hand, used satire to criticize what its editors saw as too much focus on "positive emotions" over practical solutions to Rockford's deep-seeded socioeconomic problems. They ridiculed the "Rockford math" that local politicians and civic leaders seemed to use to downplay negative statistics about our city.

If there is one thing the economic crisis of the past six years has made clear, it is that Rockfordians love their city—flaws and all. It is a love born from a sense of "going it alone." Despite holding the position of second largest city in Illinois for several decades (until being overtaken by Aurora in 2003), there is a feeling of political and economic isolation from the rest of the state. Rockford Mayor Larry Morrissey expressed this feeling in his 2012 State of the City address when he said, "Each year I have given this address, I have called us to be self-reliant as a community. We can't depend upon the State or Federal Governments to 'bail us out' or take care of our local problems," and "Tonight, I want us to think only of how we define ourselves. Let us not worry about anyone else... This is all that matters because this is our city. This is our story. This is our time."

There is a lot to be proud of in Rockford. Rockford has a rich history, a world class park district, and has been at the forefront of industrial innovation. Its neighborhoods are populated by an eclectic variety of locally owned businesses, some of which have been open for half a century or more, and local entrepreneurs have come together to make sure it remains that way. In 2010, Karen and Bob King, owners of Choices Natural Market, and Frank Schier, editor & publisher of the *Rock River Times*, created Winnebago Buy Local to promote and help grow locally-owned businesses in the area.

A rich tapestry of life, revealing our unique cultural contradictions, is being woven in the shadow of larger social and economic changes. Street gangs fight over turf to secure a piece of the international drug trade, while concerned citizens organize neighborhood groups in church basements. Real estate developers fight for government subsidies to help carve out tiny empires in the ruins of Rockford's industrial past. Mega churches like Rockford First and Heartland Community coexist alongside St. Mary Oratory, one of the few Catholic churches in the U.S. that performs the traditional Latin mass. These religious institutions share the same cultural space as a bohemian and hipster art scene, a thriving LGBT community, open street prostitution, and recreational drug markets. Local nonprofits like Rockford Rescue Mission work to give assistance to the poor, while neighboring counties release their parolees onto our streets. Our city is not only home to the Rockford Institute, an internationally-renowned paleoconservative think tank, but also Stanley Campbell's Rockford Urban Ministries. While often at odds socially, politically, and ideologically, all have contributed to contemporary life in the Forest City.

In its own way, *Secret Rockford* is both a response to Rockford's socioeconomic crisis and an attempt to "tell our story." It is unlikely that this anthology would have been created without the vigorous discussion brought on by the negative publicity Rockford has attracted in recent years. Unlike many earlier forays into the battle over Rockford's self-image, however, this anthology will confront Rockford history, politics, and culture on its own terms, without trying to sugar coat or hide unpleasant realities. This anthology is not an attempt to "market Rockford" to the outside world, but to provide a platform for the spirit of the Forest City as expressed by a variety of its residents, to preserve its history, and inform the public—particularly about issues and perspectives that are rarely discussed in our local media.

To fulfill this goal, I reached out to as many Rockford area writers, artists, and intellectuals as I could find and invited them to contribute to this anthology. Knowing that at least some of the content of *Secret Rockford* would be critical of local public policy, I even went before the city council and invited our mayor, aldermen, and city staff to contribute. I distributed our call for submissions to dozens of stores, coffee shops, and galleries in Rockford, through social media, and to more traditional media outlets. My original intent was to include a variety of fiction, nonfiction, artwork, photography, and poetry, all expressing the main theme. I received many worthwhile submissions, but what you hold in your hands right now is the best of the lot.

I would like to take this opportunity to stress that not everyone who contributed to this anthology is a professional writer. For some folks, this may be the first thing they have ever submitted for publication. All submissions have been edited for grammatical and structural considerations, but I have taken care to preserve the author's unique voice as much as possible.

This anthology contains many snapshots of life in the Forest City: a discussion of our city's reliance on Tax Increment Financing. The battle over Rockford's abortion clinic. A history of Mattison Machine Works. The story of a simple basketball game against a shoeless youth on Rockford's west side. The truth about local connections to organized crime. Infamous murders. The day Santa Claus fell from the sky. All are merely a peek behind the curtain, but each contains meaningful truths about our Rockford experience. *This* is our story. This is *Secret Rockford*.

Michael Kleen
Rock River Valley
Winter 2013/2014

ROCKFORD'S DEEPEST SECRET, BURIED UNDER EAST HIGH SCHOOL!

KAREN MAHIEU LYDDON, East High Class of 1969

East High School | Photo by Brenda Aylesworth Eisenbeisz

Rockford's oldest continuous high school, East High, sits majestically atop a hill on Charles Street. Students proudly sport East's red and black colors, and they are nicknamed the mighty E-RABS: East, Red, and Black! Construction of this spectacular school began in the spring of 1939 and was contracted to be built by U.S. Fireproofing Co. out of Chicago, along with multiple small and local subcontractors. Oh, what secrets they were to find deep below the surface!

In May 1939, the top of the hill was cut down several feet before the final building drawings were even completed. During early excavation and earthmoving, the construction crew was digging through the rich, black dirt when they ran into a large area under the northeast corner of the building where the black earth turned red. As it progressed it changed to orange-red and then struck a hard layer. The earth looked like it must have been burned.

The workers initially believed they had struck a deposit of shale when picks and shovels failed to make any progress. Subsequent heavy dynamite blasts made only slight impressions and drills bounced off the iron-like exterior. Work was then stopped while scientists from the University of Chicago visited the site and spent several days sampling and checking the area. Then, lo and behold, the scientists from Chicago and Tom Horrall, a geology instructor at Rockford Central High School, identified the material as a chunk of a meteor!

It was determined that the reddish dirt and dust was caused by metals and iron in the meteor that had rusted, while the rocks and quartz that were fused into it were blackened. The crew continued to use a combination of dynamiting and drilling to finally excavate enough to permit forms for the footings to be put in place. Explosions could be heard for miles.

After streaking through the air and lighting up the sky many ages ago, the huge meteor had struck the earth with such force that it was buried 15 feet in the ground. It must have been a spectacular sight! No signs of a crater were apparent at the time of construction. The definite size of the meteor was unknown because its discovery was limited to the footings for the new school.

However, it is assumed that the meteor that remains under East High School is of immense size.

How about those E-RABS? Their "red and black" colors were surely predestined and they do run deep under the northeast corner of the E-RAB gymnasium!

Works Cited

"Meteor Found at School Site," *Register-Star* (Rockford) 11 & 12 May 1939.

Memoirs of Forrest A. Lyddon, Supervisor of Construction for East High, West High, Washington and Lincoln Junior High Schools.

THE LOST MURAL OF
ROOSEVELT SCHOOL

ERNIE FUHR

**"Labor in Harmony" by Herbert Rosengren | From 1942
Roosevelt Junior High School Yearbook**

*"Of the artistic merit of the painting we do not attempt to speak... nor
have we any quarrel with revolutionary painting, the violent and
desperate cartoons which are supposed to represent the aspirations
of labor... But we do question whether the place for such painting is in
the schools."*

—Rockford *Morning Star* Editorial

The Lost Mural of Roosevelt School

Can junior high school students have their minds corrupted by looking at a painting? Can a work of art be so provocative that it would cause children to turn into Communists as they walk past it on the way to class every day? Apparently, there were people in Rockford who thought so. In the 1930s, a beautiful mural was displayed at Roosevelt Junior High School. If this mural still existed today, it would be nationally recognized; not only because of the artwork, but because of its place in American History. But the painting sparked controversy and "small minds" prevailed. As a result, the mural was removed and has been lost for at least 70 years. This is the story of Roosevelt School's lost mural, its controversy and the quest to find it.

To appreciate the mural, one must understand where it was located. On a personal note, I have taught at Roosevelt since 1993. I first heard about the mural many years ago, when a friend mentioned to me that it had existed. I've often said that I wouldn't want to teach anywhere else, in part because Roosevelt School is truly a neat place to go to work every day. Built in 1923, it was named after popular President Theodore Roosevelt, who had visited Rockford five times. Roosevelt School is located on Rockford's west side, at the corner of Bruce and Haskell Avenue. To this day, the building stands like a fortress in the midst of a very depressed area.

Civil engineers have rated it to be the safest, most structurally sound building in the city. On the exterior, there are two towers, four stories high, which dominate the neighborhood like beacons of hope. Above the entrances, snarling gargoyle sculptures have watched visitors come and go for over 90 years. On the interior, Roosevelt School has retained most of its original fixtures, including woodwork, marble, and mosaic tiles in the hallway. Roosevelt is the kind of public building where the walls almost "talk" to you. How appropriate that it was also home to a beautiful 12 x 14 foot mural during the New Deal era.

It was a different "President Roosevelt" who inspired the painting of the mural in 1934. That year, our country was firmly in the grip of the Great Depression. 11.3 million Americans were unemployed, 22 percent of the total labor force. In some parts of the country, unemployment was as high as 50 percent. This was an economic calamity like no other. President Franklin D. Roosevelt took unprecedented measures, invoking federal power to try to create jobs and stimulate the economy. This package of new federal agencies and job programs is commonly known as the "New Deal."

One of the earliest New Deal programs was the CWA (Civil Works Administration), which provided work in the construction trades. These were temporary, manual labor jobs, constructing and making improvements to public buildings and bridges. The CWA also oversaw a very unique program known as the PWAP (Public Works of Art Project). The mission of the PWAP was to provide work to artists, paying them to paint and beautify public buildings across America. The main criteria were that they paint the "American scene" and produce artwork that represented American values. The Roosevelt School mural, which depicted brawny workers swinging mallets, was a product of this.

The PWAP program only lasted six months, from December 1933 to June 1934, but in that brief time, the government employed 3,749 artists who produced 15,663 different works.

The Roosevelt mural was commissioned to a 26-year old artist named Herbert Rosengren. The painting was entitled "Labor in Harmony." At the top and center were three husky workers, swinging sledgehammers with their sinewy arms. Above the workers, a light beamed down from the heavens, accentuating the dignity of their labor, and trickling down to workers who labored in darkness in other sections of the painting. On the left panel, a group of workers swung mallets on a construction project. Below them were two mill workers, turning a large wheel. One of the men had his wrist shackled and his co-worker appeared to be swinging a mallet in order to break the shackle's chain against the wheel. On the right panel was a group of farm workers holding scythes, toiling in a wheat field. At the bottom of the painting, in a darker shadowy area, was a group of strikers, gathered at the point of fixed bayonets, presumably those of soldiers. To the lower left, at the "seven o'clock" position, were some coal miners. Above them, but directly below the two mill workers, there was a set of hands raised in the air, its wrists also bound in shackles. The opposite side of the painting showed another set of hands, poised to swing hand mallets. Overall, it was a very busy painting and certainly one that lived up to its title. Workers from all sectors were depicted doing their jobs triumphantly and in harmony. Yet in the lower darker regions of the painting, where workers were striking and sweating in coal mines, even being enslaved in shackles, they faced struggle and strife.

The mural was placed into position on August 6, 1934, in the hall of Roosevelt's third floor, directly facing the library. It measured 12 x 14 feet. A small brass plate was affixed at the base, noting that the painting was federal government property. A news photo in the Rockford *Register Republic* showed Mayor Henry Bloom with the artist, Herbert Rosengren as they marvel at his finished work. Just two days later, a rival newspaper wrote an editorial which leveled the first criticism of the mural.

> *"Of the artistic merit of the painting we do not attempt to speak...nor have we any quarrel with revolutionary painting, the violent and desperate cartoons which are supposed to represent the aspirations of labor...But we do question whether the place for such painting is in the schools. There is a great deal of painting that we would not put in the schools, not because it lacks value but because it creates distortion in young minds. We suggest that it be opened to view and that the parents of children who attend Roosevelt Junior Highs School, or who will attend in the next few years, be allowed to vote on whether the mural shall stand."* (Rockford *Morning Star*, August 8, 1934)

Harsher criticism of the mural came two years later, in January 1936, when Paul Kerr, representing the local American Legion Post, wrote a formal letter of complaint to the Rockford School Board. Kerr's letter charged that the mural was "communistic" and "a very poor painting for any school building." He requested that the School Board discuss the matter with the superintendent and that they have the painting removed. *"Your cooperation will be appreciated, I am sure, not only by the members*

27

of the American Legion, but by the good citizens of Rockford as well." (Rockford *Morning Star*, January 28, 1936)

What elements of the mural did Kerr and the legionnaires find objectionable? Although they were not specific about which features disturbed them, their main concern seemed to be the workers' wrists bound in shackles. This, in their opinion, was a communist theme and warranted removal.

The process by which the Legion made their judgment was an interesting one, and it did not happen overnight. In the text of his letter, Kerr explains:

> *"At the July meeting of Walter Craig Post No. 60 of the American Legion, I was appointed chairman of a committee of five, with instructions from the post and its commander to investigate the large mural painting on the wall in the upper hall of Roosevelt Junior High. That committee spent 4 months in carefully investigating the painting in question. They discussed it very thoroughly among themselves; interviewed a leading Rockford artist and also many prominent Rockford citizens, all of whom thought it was a very peculiar painting and appeared to be communistic.*
>
> *"The committee submitted a report to the Legion, to the effect that it was not the proper type of painting for any school building and that it appeared to be communistic, but they recommended that nothing further be done about it at that time. That was several months ago. Since then, I have been appointed, as a committee of one, to investigate this mural again."* (Rockford *Morning Star*, January 28, 1936)

Obviously, Mr. Kerr didn't like the mural. By consulting with a committee of like-minded people at his Legion Hall and in the citizenry, it wouldn't have been difficult to arrive at the conclusion he wanted. When no formal action was taken, Kerr wouldn't be deterred. He re-appointed himself as a "committee of one" to reinvestigate and to unilaterally demand the painting's removal.

If the Board decided to remove the painting, there would be obstacles, both legally and physically. Because the mural was federal property, Board members wondered if they would be able to remove it without getting written permission from the government. Board Attorney Charles Davis's opinion was that they could remove it if they could do so without damaging it. School Superintendent William Ankenbrand was less concerned about damaging the mural than that he was damaging the wall to which it was attached. If they removed the painting, he warned, it would be necessary to replaster and repaint the surface area.

Regarding the artwork, Superintendent Ankenbrand was not a fan, and his opinion seemed even more alarmist than others:

> *"I agree with the post that the picture is a peculiar painting, a very peculiar painting. There is a wheat field on it which is suspiciously like those one sees on posters sent out from the Soviet Republic. Without any opinion as to whether the painting is Bolshevik or not, one can look at it and say that it isn't a painting for child life. It isn't pleasing to look at. It makes one get riled up and stirred up. I didn't look at it very long. For sometimes it is too dangerous to look at some paintings too long."* (Rockford *Morning Star*, January 28, 1936)

To address the problem, School Board President Charles M. Roe appointed a special committee to investigate. The three-member committee consisted of board members Quentin Lander, Meade Durbrow, and Carl Sandstrom. Durbrow suggested that their committee meet "about a half-hour before some basketball game."

The following day, Superintendent Ankenbrand met privately with Mayor Henry Bloom to discuss the controversy. The two leaders did not reach an agreement on the painting, other than to agree to let the committee do its investigation. Although this was a closed meeting, the Rockford *Morning Star* speculated that Mayor Bloom personally liked the painting and that he opposed removal. Ankenbrand continued to be disturbed by the painting's images, saying, "*I personally think that pictures in school buildings should have happy subjects. During the formative years, children should be allowed to be happy and the sadder side of life should be hidden as much as possible."*

Ankenbrand withdrew his earlier remark about the wheat fields looking communistic, admitting, *"All wheat fields look pretty much alike, whether in the United States or Russia."*

The special committee inspected the mural for themselves. Quentin Lander, the chairman, announced that they were unable to decide whether the mural was communist inspired. However, he added that they may still order its removal, based on "general principles."

> *"If we decide that the painting contributes to the character-building processes of our educational program, we will probably recommend that it be left as it is. If it does not do this, we may suggest to the board that it be taken down, whether it appears that the charges of communism are supported or not...the painter might have the noblest motives in his work, yet produce such a screwy painting that the children would not grasp the artist's point of view."* (Rockford *Register Republic*, January 31, 1936)

The artist, Herbert Rosengren, was working in New York when he learned about the controversy. Insulted, he demanded a retraction and angrily defended his mural, denouncing the attacks as "stupid and un-American." Rosengren cleverly turned the tables on his Legion critics by offering different interpretations of the scenes he painted:

> *"By the same stretch of imagination which the Legion used in finding this mural communistic, it could be found fitting for display in an American Legion hall. The middle panel depicting marchers faced by bayonets might be described as American Legion members turned back by army bayonets in their bonus march on Washington. The big buildings in the background might represent construction the government could have carried out with money now being distributed to veterans in payment of the bonus."* (Rockford *Register Republic*, Feb. 3, 1936)

30

Rosengren explained that his artwork had been formally approved, not only by the federal government, but also by the previous school superintendent, Frank A. Jensen. Rosengren recalled that when the painting was unveiled, a school assembly was held where he explained its meaning to students. Rosengren scoffed at the idea that his farm scene resembled that of a Soviet field, saying, *"The gentleman of the schools who is capable of identifying Soviet wheat in this painting is wasting his talents. He should be an agricultural expert."* (Rockford *Register Republic*, February 3, 1936)

The Rockford chapter of the Communist Party weighed in. According to their local spokesman, David Carlen, their organization had no association with the artist. In their view, the mural was not a representation of communism. *"We agree however with the artist in that the Legion's criticism is stupid, showing that they know nothing of either communism or art. May we suggest that you give it the attention it deserves by filing it in the wastebasket."* (Rockford *Morning Star*, February 11, 1936)

The Artists Union of Chicago rallied to Rosengren's defense. They affirmed the right to freedom of speech. Likewise, they objected to the misinterpretation of the mural and opposed all efforts to remove it. They praised the art as being of "excellent decorative quality and appropriate for high school." The Artists Union sent this message via telegram to Board President Charles Roe, who then passed it along to committee chairman Quintin Lander. Coincidentally, Lander claimed to have misplaced the message, losing it in his coat pocket. As a result, it was not read at the board meeting. (Rockford *Register Republic*, February 14, 1936)

The final outcome of the dispute was a relatively simple compromise. In March 1936, the Rockford School Board decided to allow the mural to remain, but on the condition that a written explanation of the art be posted nearby. Perhaps they felt this may help viewers overcome any feelings of fear and confusion that the painting caused within them. If students had any radical impulses, reading the board's official interpretation may help them overcome such urges.

The mural lasted for a few more years. Its last known appearance was in the 1942 Roosevelt yearbook, above a caption that read, "The mural on the third floor has attracted much interest and attention." Sometime after that, the mural was quietly removed or relocated. It is hard to ascertain when that happened, as there are gaps in my personal collection of Roosevelt yearbooks. Building staff and administration from that era are now mostly deceased. An educated guess is that the mural was removed in the late 1940s or in the 1950s, a casualty of the Cold War and the Red Scare.

70 years later, the mystery remains: Where is the mural now? Is it still accessible? Initially, I assumed that it had been simply painted or plastered over. After a closer reading of the news articles, however, it became clear that it was a freestanding mural, probably painted on panels or on canvas, before being attached to the wall. In 2009, I saw a PBS television show called "History Detectives." This particular episode featured an expert in Chicago, Heather Becker, who specialized in authenticating and restoring old New Deal murals. Immediately, I wrote to Ms. Becker and shared my information with her, inviting her to investigate. I received no answer.

A year and a half passed and the trail had gone cold. In September of 2011, I wrote an ambitious proposal for our school entitled "The Roosevelt Legacy Foundation." Had this plan been supported and funded, it would have put Roosevelt "on the map" as part of the "North Main Learning Corridor" envisioned by city planners. The proposal included suggestions such as lighting the two towers of Roosevelt and more importantly, recovering our lost mural. I pointed out how restoring our mural would have been a wonderful interdisciplinary learning project to engage our high school students. The principal at the time, Mrs. Angela Hite Carter, thanked me for my ideas. She received the written proposal and promptly shelved it. Everybody has different priorities.

Another year passed. In the fall of 2012, Roosevelt School had new administration. Our new Assistant Principal was Mr.

James O'Hagan. Mr. O'Hagan is a stylish man with a zest for life and an interest in innovation. He also had many personal resources and contacts in the art community. When I told O'Hagan about our mural, he was highly interested in locating it. This was exactly the administrative support that our effort needed. O'Hagan renewed our contact with Heather Becker, the mural expert in Chicago. This time, she got back to us.

In December of 2012, when school was closed for winter break, Ms. Becker visited Roosevelt School and inspected the wall closely. She removed a cover from an exit sign and used a flashlight to examine the interior of the wall. She confirmed that the surface of the wall was solid. Our mural had not been simply painted or plastered over; it was gone. This ended our hopes of peeling back layers of paint and plaster in order to recover a painting beneath. Becker's inspection yielded a couple of other clues. She found evidence of framing and two square nails still embedded in the top of the wall.

The next phase involved searching old storage areas. If the mural was a rolled-up canvas, it would have to be at least 12 feet long. If it were painted on boards, it would also be rather cumbersome, requiring a great deal of space. Mr. O'Hagan searched the school's attic and looked in the basement and adjoining tunnels. He didn't find it in either of these places.

To publicize our efforts, we started a Facebook page called "Friends of the Roosevelt Mural." This allowed us to tell the story of the mural and gather leads to its whereabouts. A former staffer wrote that it was relocated to a wall in a nearby office on the third floor. He claimed that during renovations, another wall had been built over the mural, concealing it. I found this intriguing, and when I looked at the office in question, it seemed plausible. I didn't pursue it because I think it would be tacky to go around knocking holes in the walls, especially if the room is used for conferences or as somebody's office.

Currently, we are no closer to discovering Roosevelt's lost mural. I am thankful that we have been able to pick up a few clues over the years. I recently learned that the Rockford School Board has kept archives of all their records and minutes, dating back to the early 1900s. They have granted me permission to browse them for the time frames in question. Hopefully, their archives will provide new information. If not, I will still enjoy examining the original correspondence and documentation from 1936.

The quest for a historical artifact is like the quest for learning: It is a long process which may require a great deal of patience and persistence. Even if we fall short of the ultimate goal, it is fun to discover new things along the way and to share that knowledge with others.

Works Cited

1942 Roosevelt Junior High Yearbook, Rockford, IL. The mural is pictured on page 16. On an unrelated note, also pictured in this yearbook is an 8th grader named Evelyn Almond, the mother of actress Jodie Foster.

Smithsonian American Art Museum: A New Deal for Artists http://americanart.si.edu/exhibitions/archive/2009/1934/

New Deal Art Registry, www.newdealartregistry.org

"School Board Gets Sketches of 2 Paintings: CWA Employs Artists for Junior High Murals," *Morning Star* (Rockford) 6February 1934.

"New PWA Mural Inspected by Mayor Bloom," *Register Republic* (Rockford) 7 August 1934.

"Rebel Art," editorial, *Morning Star* (Rockford) 8 August 1934.

"Claim Painting Communistic; Ask Removal: Rosengren Mural on Junior High Wall Criticized," *Morning Star* (Rockford) 28 January 1936.

"Artists Rally To Defense of School Mural," *Register Republic* (Rockford) 28 January 1936.

"Bloom and Ankenbrand Confer on 'Red' Mural," *Morning Star* (Rockford) 29 January 1936.

"School Board May Banish PWA Mural 'On General Principles'," *Register Republic* (Rockford) 31 January 1936.

"Artist Replies to Charge That School Mural is Communistic," *Register Republic* (Rockford) 3 February 1936.

"Reds Decline to Own Mural: Urge Legion Protest to Be Consigned to Wastebasket," *Morning Star* (Rockford) 11 February 1936.

"Artists Union Defends Mural in School Here," *Register Republic* (Rockford) 14 February 1936.

"Mural to Remain On School Wall," *Morning Star* (Rockford) 24 March 1936.

"The Passing Day," Editorial, *Morning Star* (Rockford) 25 March 1936.

MATTISON MACHINE WORKS

WORKS

THE LIFE AND DEATH OF AN AMERICAN LEGEND

HEATH D. ALBERTS

The Rockford Metropolitan Area has long been known world-wide as being a veritable treasure trove of industry, engineering ingenuity, and mechanical aptitude. During the Cold War, Rockford had the ominous distinction of being at the top-heavy end of the 'first strike' list, due solely to the importance brought to bear in the singular manufacturing and machining prowess that it offered up to the world at home, and at large, on a daily basis.

Among the names of the giants who once dwelled in Rockford (and some that still do) reside a veritable *Who's Who* of industry; a snapshot of industrial goliaths known and respected world-wide. Tangled in amongst these was a somewhat lesser-known, but no less important, name: *The Mattison Machine Works.*

In understanding a company's greatness, one often finds oneself inquiring about its roots. Certainly, in the light of the here and now, anyone can see what it has become—what it means to the society that has come to depend upon its products, whether directly or indirectly. Even still, every story has a beginning. And this one in particular, I felt, was well worth sharing.

◆   ◆   ◆

The Mattison Machine Works found its humble beginnings not in Rockford, but an ocean away in the country of Norway. More specifically, in the form of a young Norwegian native named Chris Mattison. In 1870, Mattison had blossomed into a hyper-intelligent fourteen year old. Like many young men of his age he was ambitious and had big dreams of one day making a fortune, and subsequently a lasting mark, upon a society at large who knew nothing of him in the here and now. Little did he know at that tender age how impactful—and lasting—that mark would become.

With his head brimming with inspired caprice, it was almost inevitable that Mattison found himself voyaging upon a sail-laden vessel, on his way to the proverbial land of opportunity: America. After a mercifully uneventful voyage, he disembarked for the first time upon the hallowed soil of America. This successful return to terra firma immediately forced a young Mattison to make his second, life-changing decision in answer to the question: *Now what?*

For Mattison, we can only assume that the question, as it might for any one of us in his place, carried a great deal of weight. Here was a young man bent on mental stimulation, and on learning all that anyone cared to teach him. He was ambitions, able-bodied, nimble-minded, and willing to take on any task in order to show what he was made of.

In the end, Mattison selected the then-booming industry of woodworking. We once more find record of him in 1872, at the age of sixteen, where he was by then gainfully employed by a chair factory in Minneapolis, Minnesota. His foremost skill, at this time, seems to have been the art of bending chair backs in a difficult to master, artisanal manner; a method which had been handed down from master to apprentice for decades.

Fourteen years, and a great many mastered experiences, later we once more find record of Mattison as having expertly mastered the production and manufacturing processes associated not only with chairs, but with doors, sash, and other wood products then utilized by builders nationwide. In recognition of his efforts and acuity, he was placed at the head of one of the largest woodworking plants in Minneapolis at the time. At the age of thirty, he had made something remarkable of himself, even having filed patents for both wood cutting heads, and specific machines, developed for the manufacture of wood products. For most individuals this, in and of itself, would signify a meaningful life well spent. For Chris Mattison, it marked the beginning of far greater things to come.

◆　　◆　　◆

Instead of sitting proudly on his laurels—an act which he had already well earned—Mattison made the bold choice to strike out on his own, pull up stakes, and move to another manufacturing

Mecca. And so, in 1896, Mattison found himself in Beloit, Wisconsin. Here, after founding *C. Mattison Machine Works,* he worked diligently and feverishly in hatching and refining rudimentary thoughts and concepts into working and functional machinery and tooling. These came with innovations the likes of which the woodworking industry had never witnessed before (and some, to this day, revered by purists as the best ever offered by anyone, at any time). Mattison was charting new territory, and he was nowhere near finished. He continued to innovate, and patent, new cutters, designs, methods and—most importantly—entire machines for the industrial woodworking industry. Across America, woodwork tycoons and workers alike must have, one can only imagine, rejoiced at these new-found methods and products which made their product more inexpensive to manufacture, while making the lives of the operators far less difficult.

With all of the aforementioned in mind, one might be inclined to think that Mattison had nothing but a plethora of success, and one would be half right in doing so. The harsh reality, however, was less rosy. Like any business owner, Mattison had put his future—and his livelihood—on the line in founding a business of his own. While he was permitted to revel in its successes, he was also most impacted by its failings, and the difficulties and challenges that came with owning a business founded on cutting-edge innovation. While not specifically documented, numerous sources point to the fact that these years of triumph were littered with crushing defeats, and significant financial and intellectual hurdles as well.

By this time, however, Mattison had married and had two sons who were now on the cusp of working age. To ease his own burden, he embraced his two boys—A.M. Mattison and C.L. Mattison—as the potential future of this meaningful endeavor which he had so proudly founded. With their assistance, Mattison went on to develop new additions to his already impressive offerings. These included innovative new designs in lathes—specifically turning, propeller, and reproducing types. Also on offer were new sawing and sanding machines. It was also at this point that Mattison began a new venture into the world of metalworking.

It began with shapers, but his legacy with regard to this fateful decision can still be felt, even to this day.

◆ ◆ ◆

With the addition of his sons to the day-to-day operations of the business, and the exponential growth his new ideas and concepts were bringing to bear, Mattison made yet another bold move. Realizing that he was soon going to suffer space constraints in his current location, he scouted for potential new sites for a custom-built plant to house the next phase of his business. In the end, Mattison selected another industrial juggernaut in which to put down roots: Rockford, Illinois.

The early months of 1918 saw the completion of his new facility at 545 Blackhawk Park Avenue, and Mattison wasted no time in expanding his offerings in the metalworking field. From the confines of this new facility, numerous purpose-specific machines were designed, developed, and built. Most notably were tube grinders, polishing machines, abrasive belt grinders, moulding machines, and—to my way of thinking—the most important and lasting contribution of all: the surface grinder (more on that in a bit).

By 1910, Mattison had built a small empire. At this point in his life, he elected to settle down a bit more, and in a bold move handed over the reins of company oversight. Even so, he still retained the title of president up until the time of his death in 1920.

With his father's passing, A.M. Mattison was chosen to take the helm of the company as president. During this period, in the early first-third of the twentieth century, Mattison's machines most prominently served in the manufacturing of the wood bodies of automobiles. With the innovational advent of the 'turret-top' automobile body, however, the Mattisons could see the writing on the wall clearly enough. Like any significant legacy company they re-evaluated their offerings, and were nimble enough to change with the times. As such, a more sincere bent was placed on the development of new and innovative metalworking machine designs. This was done not only to continue to serve this core industry, but to also permit the *Mattison* name to branch out further into new fields of sales potential.

Of these innovative new developments, one stands out amongst all others: the precision horizontal-spindle reciprocating table surface grinder. *Mattison Machine Works*, for all of its wonders and successes, is best known for this specific product; a product that, in many machine shops across the globe, is still in use—even today. Parts for these machines are still made to order (or even stocked) with regularity. They are still sold—often daily—by the now-owners of the rights to the line, *Bourn & Koch Machine Tool*, located on Kishwaukee Avenue in Rockford, Illinois. Amazingly, *Bourn & Koch* is located only blocks from the original *Mattison Machine Works* plant.

As the years rolled on, the company seemed unstoppable. Even so, like so many other companies of every shape, size, and sort, nothing could have prepared them for the unique trials foisted upon them—and all of America—by the Great Depression. Even a company as profoundly important and innovative as *Mattison* was not immune.

The Great Depression had the unfortunate knack of having a 'trickle-down' effect upon businesses, and *Mattison* was no exception. Rockford, at this time, was a furniture manufacturing powerhouse. When the demand for furniture began to wither on the vine of prosperity, so too did the demand for machinery, aftermarket components, and labor associated with its manufacture. While Rockford provided a profoundly solid location with regard to rail and truck transportation, many furniture makers consolidated (if they managed to remain in business at all) to southeastern states. This hurt the entire Rockford area, but it hurt *Mattison* even more.

Through these hard years, A.M. Mattison focused even more on the transition from woodworking machines to metalworking machines, until his passing in 1938. Business during these difficult years proved to be full of high and low fluctuations, often to the point of randomness. Even so, continued innovation and improvement occurred and the business not only survived, but even expanded to a small degree.

With A.M. Mattison's passing, his brother C.L. Mattison grasped the reins and continued to lead the company from the financial wreckage until his death in 1948. The company became even more of a family affair, when Chris Mattison's grandsons began serving in corporate leadership and steering capacities: Alan C. Mattison served as Secretary, Phillip L. Mattison served as Treasurer, and Ronald W. Mattison served as Vice President.

As the Great Depression drew further and further toward a cessation, *Mattison Machine Works* found itself uniquely situated to assist with—and capitalize upon—the next major page in America's history: World War II. This was the first recorded time when *Mattison* grinders truly showed their stuff. They became indispensable tools in the production of wartime necessities, most notably aircraft components, machine tools, and arsenal products.

During this time, *Mattison Machine Works* was known for implementing some unique business ideas as well. Foremost among them were the development of their own casting facility (so as not to be reliant, nor beholden, to a vendor for this crucial service), and a workers' dormitory. Sadly, both were severely damaged in a massive inferno that befell them in the fall of 1946. To the relief of all concerned, the foundry's master patterns were unscathed. While not the best of situations, it still permitted outlying foundries to continue to pour the much-needed and critical cast components off-site, using these surviving master patterns. During this time, it has also been noted, that *Mattison* went to great lengths to make certain that its foundry employees remained gainfully employed, by either moving them to different departments within the company, or securing them employment with the foundries now pouring the critical castings.

With a great deal of effort and diligence, the foundry was brought back into service in a mere six month period. With the advent of this new facility, all of its original employees were once more returned to their rightful place, and in-house casting production was officially begun anew, by March of 1947.

One year later, C.L .Mattison passed away. With his passing, Alan C. Mattison escalated to the position of President, while Phil Mattison made the move to Vice President, and Ronald Mattison served as Secretary.

In 1949, the company made a major acquisition of the rights to the entire line of rotary and surface grinders that were then being produced by *Hatchett Manufacturing Co.* in Big Rapids, Michigan. What this acquisition brought with it was the ability to further enable *Mattison Machine Works* to solidify itself as a tier-one supplier in both the agricultural and automotive industries.

A second major acquisition came again in December of 1956. This time, *Mattison* absorbed the Milwaukee, Wisconsin-based *Mercury Engineering Co.,* a producer of precision grinding machinery. This acquisition permitted them the unique opportunity to develop, and ultimately offer for sale, a foundry grinder. This new grinder was designed to grind both the joint surfaces, and the deck faces, of engine blocks as they arrived from the foundry. Another viable niche-market had been filled by the ever-increasing product line on offer at *Mattison Machine Works.*

In 1960, engineers within *Mattison* developed a new design for a planetary grinding head (a head that turns, as sub-heads also turn in kind). The benefits of this new offering were numerous, but the most important of these was the increase in versatility and capabilities with regard to rotary-style grinders. This new addition to their already impressive line turned a number of industry heads, and further offered up new inroads into serving new clients, and business models.

It was also around this time that the company set its sights on something far more ambitious than anything that they had undertaken to date: international sales. With a solid belief that their product was superior to a vast majority available (it was), and also in possession of some proprietary wonders that otherwise were not available anywhere, *Mattison* began to test the international waters.

By 1963, a licensing agreement had been reached with *Koyo Machine Company Limited* in Japan. This blossomed further into a full-blown, joint venture called *Koyo-Mattison, Ltd.* in 1973. This symbiotic relationship was a boon for the company, and it opened the door to subsequent inroads in both Taiwan, and Italy as well.

In 1982, a changing of the guard occurred once again, with the passing of Alan Mattison. This brought Phil Mattison to the helm, while elevating Ronald Mattison to Vice-Presidency, Arthur Mattison to Secretary, and Ronald Mattison, Jr. to Assistant Secretary.

Though the loss was great, the designers, developers, and engineers at *Mattison* continued to do what they did best: innovate. As such, they developed new ways to expand their double-disc and corrugated roll grinding machines.

A scant two years thereafter, Phil Mattison passed away, and a transfer of power once more occurred. Even with another death in the family, *Mattison* continued to seek to better itself. With this in mind, they made another significant acquisition, in the form of *Hitachi-Magnalock*, which inspired and blossomed into the *Magna-Lock USA* line of pneumatic work holding devices and magnetic chucks. With the addition of these two new technologies, *Mattison* once more proved that—as a collective whole—it was a company bent on innovation and industry diversity, and one that certainly knew what it was doing.

Mattison also took this early opportunity to embrace a new form of radical change. This came not in the purchase of an additional company, nor the development of a new technology. Rather, it came in the form of the embracing of *AutoCAD*, a relatively new product which permitted acetate, and hand drawings, to become a thing of the past. This, in time, elevated the abilities of the engineering staff to levels of efficiency and ability unseen up to that point.

While the addition of *AutoCAD* was a stunning move, they hedged their bets on the coming age of technology one step further by implementing micro-computers and terminals in key areas, to further increase the productivity and abilities of support staff.

Finally, *Mattison* chose to acquiesce to the future in the most difficult way: by adding technology to the machines themselves. After more than three-quarters of a century of innovation, CNC (computer numeric controls), and process controllers, were being integrated into their product line offering.

The remainder of the 1980s saw the company furthering its reach into the industries in which it already played a dominant role. It also saw the discontinuation of a significant portion of its woodworking machinery group. One can't help but wonder how Chris Mattison would have felt about this move. Given his astute mind, and comprehension of an ever-changing business world, one hopes that he would have agreed with the soundness of the decision. By this point, *Mattison* had been offering machines to the world for a phenomenal stretch of time. This resulted in a hefty source of aftermarket income rolling into their coffers, in the form of add-on accessories, repair parts, and field service.

By 1993, the winds of change were blowing. In August, a new corporate structure was initiated. P.L. Mattison, Jr. took the helm for the final two years of operation, from 1993-1995. When operations finally ceased in 1995, more than 8,000 grinders, and 16,000 woodworking machines had been delivered into a world which craved—and needed—the technologies and innovations brought to bear by this manufacturing giant.

Rights to the machine line, and more importantly the aftermarket parts and service, were sold to *DeVlieg-Bullard Services Group* in Machesney Park, Illinois. Upon their bankruptcy, the company was restructured, and became known as *DeVlieg-Bullard II*. Upon subsequent bankruptcy proceedings, some years later, the rights to the line were sold to *Bourn & Koch Machine Tool* of Rockford. To this day, local machine shops continue to make aftermarket components for these machines. The reason? The quality and longevity instilled into the making and design of these machines were such that they remain a revered name among their operators. In point of fact, a good number of these machines still reside, and create revenue for, a large number of Rockford businesses and families.

In April 2010, the *Mattison Machine Works* building suffered an estimated $300,000 in damage when an employee of then-tenant, *Production Machinery Company, Inc.*, accidentally set fire to the structure while using an acetylene torch. Nevertheless, the building still exists to this day.

◆   ◆   ◆

In the aftermath of writing this, I felt a compelling need to convey the *why* of the thing. Why choose this company to write about for an anthology about Rockford? In its simplest form, the answer is: personal reverence. For the past sixteen years, I have worked as the operations manager of a local contract manufacturing machine shop. Over those years, I have dealt with many former employees of *Mattison*. Most notably Mr. Paul Allen, who graciously provided much of the historical data which was unavailable anywhere else except within the *Mattison Machine Works* corporate archives, now in the possession of *Bourn & Koch Machine Tool*. These documents made this work a reality that it could not have otherwise been.

Over these years, I have seen thousands of blueprints from all of the machines in the *Mattison* lines—woodworking and metalworking alike. As the individual who is responsible for the quoting of potential work for our business, it is my job to review these drawings in an effort to establish price for the customer. I've seen drawings dating as far back as the 1920s—meaning that someone out there is still using that machine, or I wouldn't be receiving a request for quotation to manufacture the desired replacement parts. That, frankly, awed me to no end. *Mattison* almost inexplicably developed products so singularly well-made, as to be ahead of their time in many ways. The proof of this is in the number of machines that, based on my experience, are still in use to this day.

Their drawings and blueprints were also quite singular in nature. Specifically, they have the unique tendency to not only express how to manufacture the desired component, they also provide additional data, indicating what mating part goes where. This is an innovation that, to this day, I have seen on no other drawings from any of the more than five-hundred machine lines which have crossed my desk over the years. It is particularly ingenious, in that it prevents one from needing to see—and decipher—an assembly drawing. Instead, if something requires changing, or a question is posed, it is a simple matter to find—and change—the appropriate part in a short period of time.

Their legacy doesn't end there, either. I have been to dozens of local shops and grinding houses that still use these machines every day, and speak of them as a pious person might of Christ himself. They do this for no other reason than that they feel *compelled* to. The machinery is simply too demanding of this sort of reverence to be denied its rightful due.

As I've stood before different makes, models, and years of these machines, one thing begins to become clear (likewise in the drawings, to some degree): these machines are often elegant works of mechanical art. The time, care, love, passion, and ingenuity that went into bringing them to life is evident, even in the most simple of components. Even so, the simplest of components stemmed from a diligent refining of possibilities, pared down to their core essentials of usefulness and cost. It's a study in humility when one observes the machine as it runs and does its work before your very eyes.

Before *Bourn & Koch* purchased the physical and intellectual property rights to this line, I was once afforded the opportunity to visit the 'print room' at *DeVlieg-Bullard Services Group.* The room seemed as long as it was high and wide—the word 'enormous' doesn't even begin to describe it. I was told that it housed more than three million blueprints. Inclusive within all of these machinery line prints, were the *Mattisons.* I imagined, for a moment, all of the lives that had made what was before me possible. All of those engineers, many now long dead, whose artistic work was initialed or signed, in blueprints dating back more than a century. Their legacy—specifically recalled or not—resided in that room. It was beyond humbling.

A number of years back I received a call from a friend of mine, Mr. Norm Keinz. Norm is also a Rockford staple, as he is the owner and founder of *Security Alarm Co.* I have known him for decades, and have assisted him with small projects within his business from time to time, mostly on the computer side of things. On this particular occasion, however, he had a unique request: could I assist him in setting up some long-range motion lasers in a huge building? That building, it turned out, was the old *Mattison Machine Works*, sitting vacant. I still remember—to this day—walking in, and just stopping in my tracks. This place—this shrine to machining excellence and a family business from beginning to end—was where many of those machines had come from.

It might sound foolish, but I actually found myself tearing up. Thankfully, Norm was already at the other end of the building, and didn't see the spontaneous emotional outpouring. Here, within these walls, all of those dedicated men and women had worked in unison to produce something magnificent; something far more than any one of them could have made possible on their own. The sheer immensity of the place set me to imagining it, in my mind, when it was in full swing. It still brings out genuine emotions as I consider it, even now. Somehow I'd like to think that Chris Mattison approved of my comportment and reverence for his legacy, as I stood within the temple to industry those hallowed walls represented.

Works Cited

"*Brief History,*" Received From Mr. Paul Allen, *Bourn & Koch Machine Tool* Archives, Rockford, Illinois.

"*History Of The Company—Document # 14733-1/6-20-97,*" Received From Mr. Paul Allen, *Bourn & Koch Machine Tool* Archives, Rockford, Illinois (20 June 1997).

"Blaze at former Mattison building causes $300K in damage," *Register Star* (Rockford) 27 April 2010.

Havens, Joel (12 December 2013). "*Mattison Machine Works,*" http://vintagemachinery.org/mfgindex/detail.aspx?id=357.

A DARK WOOD

D. B. LANE

"Midway through the journey of our life, I found myself within a dark wood, for the right way had been lost."

—Dante's *Divine Comedy*

He sat in the black, battered old Ford, squeezing the worn steering wheel until his clenched knuckles became cramped and bloodless. Still gripping, he leaned forward enough to peer up through the dirty, cracked windshield, and muttered, "Looks like it might rain after all." He cringed, not for talking out loud—he'd actually been doing that a lot lately—but because it conjured an image of Abel, sneering and flicking his head smartly with a wink like he always used to do, and saying something smart-ass like, "*Is that what you're really worried about at a time like this, Jackie?*" A smile tried to rise to Jack's lips, but it faded when the picture of cocky, ambling Abel floated away before his watery eyes.

Having dressed up in his Sunday best, he'd driven his father's decrepit automobile from Midlin Township to Forrest City. Those thirty bumpy miles along old Grant Road used to be part of a stage line running west all the way to Galena and the Mississippi. A railroad ran parallel to it now, hauling passengers and freight as far east as Chicago and the Stockyards. As youngsters, he and Abel had stumbled on old man Huber's still and got tanked on his family's recipe for "medicinal" spirits. Then they'd scrambled into a slow-moving freight car, thinking it would be a romantic adventure, but the real hobos had flung them off before they'd reached the Windy City. And all they'd wanted to do was to stand a little while on what Sandburg called those Big Shoulders.

It had been more than a two day walk back; two days missing farm work, the first spent sick and hung over and the second fearful and hungry. They'd had every reason to be frightened, too: Papa knew just where to find the most supple yet unforgiving wood in the deepest, darkest parts of the forest, and he stripped and whittled until he had fashioned a razor-fine switch. The boys stood at meals and church for a good two weeks and never pulled a stunt like that again.

Now here he sat, in a suit with sleeves too short and ten years out of style, enveloped in descending twilight, waiting for closing time. Why in heaven's name had he dressed up in the only suit coat and tie he owned? Had he really harbored thoughts of breezing in and having a meeting, some business-like tete-a-tete with the manager or the vice-president maybe?

Although it wasn't a huge, thriving metropolis like Chicago, somehow Forrest City unnerved him, making Midlin seem like an inconsequential, fly-swatting backwater. Those thirty miles felt interminable, like crossing the deserts of the wandering Jews. He hoped now, though, that his problems wouldn't seem so bad in electric lights and business suits.

But then he inhaled the car's fetid odor of farm work and the reek of country life that had permeated his skin and hardened his heart; it was a stench of three-day-old sweat, corn squeezings, and manure. He couldn't get the shit out from under his fingernails if he pried them off with his teeth. His clothes were as ratty and worn as he was. They didn't make him look smart or neat, they just made him feel cheap and stupid.

And Jack Foster was tired of being both.

The clock was ticking. In another half-hour, it would be done. The glowering winter sun went down early these days, so it would be all but dark in a little while; chilly without the motor running, but at least there wasn't any snow or bitter winds yet.

Just then a rap on the window made Jack lurch in his seat. A cop was bent down by the driver's side. Jack strained against the bent window crank.

"Everything all right, buddy?"

"Yes, sir. Just waiting for my brother." Jack jerked his head towards the barber shop a few doors back.

The cop looked him over silently. "Thought maybe you was stalled. It'd be warmer if you was to wait in the shop, don't you think?"

Jack mentally groped for an answer and was hoping the cop wouldn't notice the cap lying on the passenger side. He could always say it was his brother's, which wasn't a lie, and that Abel had left it in the car when he went in to get his hair cut. Jack was more worried about the burlap sack next to it and its contents. That would be harder to explain. Then he wondered what might happen if the cop went to look in the barber shop.

"I don't get on so good with my brother anymore."

The weary policeman just shrugged, tugging his coat collar tighter around his throat. "Well, if you're sure you're all right now. Tony'll be closing soon," he said, throwing a thumb over his shoulder. He tapped on the car's warm hood as he went on with his beat, not bothering to look back.

"Damn," Jack drawled, making it one long, low syllable. He rolled up the window, pulling the scratchy cloth from his red, itching neck. When he glanced at his father's tarnished pocket watch, he sighed: twenty more minutes. In the wedge of the rearview mirror, he noticed the store next to the barber's with the three balls above the torn and splotchy awning. He fleetingly thought of pawning the watch, but then his eyes locked on the bank building ahead, already in shadow, like some hungry predator pretending to sleep.

It began to rain, and Jack allowed it to smear and obscure his view, hoping it would wash the bugs and grime from the windshield. The thin cracks in the glass spread like tentacles, reaching across the driver's side from a pockmark where Abel had hit it with a baseball years ago. Another smile was squashed under the memory of poverty so severe that it had prevented fixing or replacing the glass. Thank heaven the windshield held. Now the cracked glass remained like Abel's handprint on a frosty window pane, lasting long after the warm flesh was gone.

He slammed his fist on the dash. "Stop taunting me!" he screamed, the windows filming over with his breath. He slumped and let his aching hand fall to the bench seat. "Please, stop reminding me," he pleaded much more quietly. He didn't bother to start the engine to run the wipers. They didn't work well, and he wouldn't be needing them anyway.

Somehow, the rain brought memories of Papa Luther and stories of leaving the beloved, wet moors of his youth to come to a new world. He'd built the farm with the help of his father, Douglass, their labor cutting the trees from the thick, dark woods and fashioning the house, the barn, the chicken coops and pens. Soon, Jack's father John came along, and it was his and Luther's sweat that tended the livestock and plowed the fields. *Blood is thicker than water, boy-o,* Papa had always said, and Jack had never understood that as a child. But he smiled now remembering his grandfather's warmth, the rumbling laugh and huge, rough hands on his thin, sloping shoulders.

He also recalled another, darker dream: how Grandma Lorraine's father had made a rocking chair from the dark, heavy forest wood, the last piece of furniture he crafted in this country before he died. Although Jack was older and they both knew better, he and Abel had been roughhousing on the chair. Abel always had to butt heads with his older brother, go further and push beyond the limits. Both of the chair's rockers cracked and splintered under their weight, and the whole thing crashed, boys' arms and legs splaying to the sound of doomsday. Jack took the blame and it culminated in another "woodshed" moment that he wouldn't soon forget, though he never told on Abel.

Mostly, though, his childhood was dotted with vistas of tightly woven woods broken only by the seasonal turnings of brown, fallow fields to hard crusted, untainted snow. At other times, it seemed like magic when the land sprouted vast stretches of corn or lush prairie plains flowing with tall wild grass spreading like fingers reaching for the ends of the earth.

Just then, thunder rippled like a waking beast, bringing him back to the street-lit Ford hunched just a few blocks from the behemoth that ultimately controlled his fate. It stood, an imposing figure like the giant Goliath—the evil Mammon that held the lien against his family's property.

The wind had picked up and blew the increasing rain in splashing gusts. The red and white swirls of the barber's pole were still hypnotizing blurs in the rearview mirror, but in fifteen minutes or so that would cease as Tony closed up. Jack thought of the farm where, as the firstborn son, he'd worked alongside Papa and his father through all kinds of foul weather like this. That is, until Abel came along. After a stillborn baby and a little sister, Louise, who'd died as an infant, his mother became quiet and distant, wrapped up with the garden, the chickens, and the house. It fell to Jack to keep up with his chores and tend little Abel, which left precious little time for anything else, not that he went to school much or had many friends.

The late season thunderstorm cleared its throat. The windows had fogged up, but Jack couldn't even crack one because of the incessant rain. When it turned to hail, banging on the car's metal, it sounded like gunfire. Abel's war tales came to mind unbidden, and Jack closed his eyes, trying to force them out, willing them to stop their relentless replay but to no avail. After Luther had died, Abel had run off to join the Great War. Jack was just past having a young man's heart, and stomach, so he'd stayed home to help his father with the farm and care for his ailing mother. After all, blood was thicker than water.

Abel didn't have enough brawn for the infantry, but he longed to become a pilot, and he had been a good one. He had always claimed, with a wink and a flick of his head, that it was all due to bravery and daring. Jack thought it more likely a matter of blind, stupid luck. Either way, Abel had returned to Illinois a hero of sorts, not with any medals to show for it, but just for returning alive without symptoms of shell-shock, mustard gas, or missing limbs. Being a cocky, good-looking flier made him a stand-out, especially with the girls.

It was supposed to have been the war to end all wars, but it didn't end their troubles at home. When their mother succumbed to the influenza, John became brooding and withdrawn, losing weight he couldn't afford and growing weaker. This threw almost all of the farm's burdens on Jack's shoulders since Abel's solution was to make money crop-dusting. When that venture failed, he found it more lucrative to smuggle booze. During the Prohibition, local and federal law enforcement were cracking down on rum-runners by sea and bootleggers by land, but not many were aware of, or smart enough to catch, the high-fliers like Abel Foster.

Jack winced at the clattering roof and the simultaneous lightning flash with the thunder's heavy roll. His hand slid to the burlap sack for comfort. Abel would have sneered that Jack was getting jumpy as he got older; what was he now, thirty-three, or was it thirty-five? His stubbly chin and sunken, sallow cheeks in the mirror showed a haggard face reminiscent of his father, though twenty years sooner than his old man had worn that much care.

Grandma Lorraine had always said, *You're only as old as you feel, Jackie boy*, which did him no good since he looked like hell and felt older than Papa, father, and mama combined, like he'd been in the grave twice as long as they'd all been dead. And how old would Abel be now? Twenty-eight, or was it thirty? God, he couldn't even remember Abel's birthday, or his own, for that matter. How long had it been since he'd celebrated anyone's birthday, or a holiday? He couldn't recall Luther's or John's birth dates either. Everything was slipping. Grinding his teeth, he started to bawl. *Oh, for cryin' out loud, Jack,* Abel would've growled, but then, chuckling: *Hey, ya get it? "For cryin' out loud!" Come on, Jackie, that's funny!* . . .

"Shut up, Ace, just shut up!" This had always been Jack's derogatory term for his kid brother, but one that Abel seemed to relish, flicking his head and laughing. Screaming this now, as it echoed in the closed car, stopped his tears but intensified the throbbing behind his closed eyes. He blindly reached to finger the cap. When he tried to picture his mother's face, he couldn't recall a single feature, and he wept again.

Glancing at his father's watch, he saw that time was almost up. The barber pole went black, and Tony's shadow locked the door from inside. When the lights were extinguished, old Tony probably shambled up some steep, narrow steps to a little cold-water flat that he shared with a fat, blind cat. Some life, huh Tony?

More jagged electricity streaked above the bank. Abel, persistent little bastard that he'd always been, came knocking back at Jack's weary senses. Jack had a clear vision of the exact moment, by the old kitchen stove over morning coffee, when Abel had proudly announced to his father and brother that he was going "legit." He was going to be a barnstormer.

Though John was stoic, Jack was livid. When the angry words, and those left unsaid, finally settled, Abel was off to be a daredevil, looping and diving with his ramshackle biplane. He even bragged about heading for California to put his stunts in moving picture shows, but he never made it. He wound up roasting alive in a fireball one dreary, overcast Sunday in Des Moines. There wasn't much left of the plane and nothing of Abel to bury. The only thing thrown clear was Abel's military cap, which he always wore when flying, so Jack kept it.

They'd had a funeral with a beautiful coffin that John had fashioned from a dark wood very reminiscent of that ancient broken rocking chair. It was the last thing he'd ever put together on this earth. They'd placed a photograph of Abel and some personal things in the casket, but Jack kept the cap and never said a word about it.

It had rained at the service, almost like it was pouring now, and John had not only refused an umbrella from Jack, but he'd also given his coat to an elderly woman from the United Methodist Ladies' Auxiliary. He contracted double pneumonia, and some days later, the doctors said he suffered an acute attack of angina. What the hell kind of jargon was that? Jackie knew better: his old man was worn out and died of desperation and longing before he reached sixty.

As usual, Jack was left to pick up the pieces and shoulder on, only now there weren't too many pieces left. When the Crash hit, Jack and the farm limped along, but he felt increasingly like he thought his father must have felt towards the end: old, tired, and defeated. The bank bore down, but Jack couldn't stand to just let everything go that his family had struggled so hard to build. Blood is, in the end, thicker than water.

That's when Jack thought of trying to work out a plan with them. Bankers were reasonable business people after all, and human beings with families and children, too. They'd certainly want to help Jack succeed rather than just allow him to fail. But that did not seem to be the case. They were adamant, insisting that if Jack defaulted, they would foreclose, seize the property and take everything.

That's how Jack wound up here as a last resort. If reason wouldn't work, then he'd concocted some silver-screen fantasy about dressing up nice, like Capone or Dillinger, and charging into the bank just before closing time to rob from the rich and run like hell, maybe head for California. That's why he'd brought the sack: it contained a revolver that Luther had always claimed his father Douglass was given as a gift by Buffalo Bill himself at a Wild West show before the turn of the century. There was also Abel's military handgun, and one of those newfangled, gas-powered automatic weapons that he swore he'd taken when he shot a German officer. Jack figured that if you can't find any other solution, then maybe it's time to blast your way out. It worked for Cagney and Edward G.

Now though, Jack had formulated a different plan. So he waited until the bank closed, the lights were shut off, and all the employees had left, locking the door, yelling good night to each other as they ran to their cars, trying not to get soaked. He waited a few more minutes and thought about Papa and John and the farm. He had an image of old Tony and his fat, blind cat getting their sleep disturbed. He wondered if that beat cop was due back around, or maybe he was off home, sitting down to a hot supper with the missus, snuggling up to the radio to be lulled by one of those fireside chats about fear itself. He remembered his inscrutable, distant mama, the stillborn baby, and poor little Louise, too. Mostly he pictured Abel and wondered that his scrappy little brother hadn't come up with this idea sooner.

Jack took off his hat and, tossing it into the back, picked up the cap and tenderly placed it on his head. It was a little small, though, so smiling and flicking his head, he flipped it off and returned it at a jaunty angle. Looking at himself in the mirror, he almost laughed, wondering how that could make him look and feel at least ten years younger, but it did.

"Much better, Ace. You're only as old as you feel, kiddo."

He started the engine and let it idle. The old car rumbled like Abel's beat-up plane. Jack had never ridden in an airplane, though Abel had offered to take him up on numerous occasions. He gunned the gas pedal a few times, the old Ford's motor groaning and growling with fury, and then put it into gear, not bothering to turn on the wiper blades.

Although he'd certainly never flown an airplane, somehow Jack was certain that he could get this old jalopy airborne and take off right through that bank window. When he floored the accelerator and sped down State Street, he saw visions of that dark, wooden rocking chair just before it collapsed, spilling him and Abel on the ground, and his brother's empty casket being lowered into a black, fathomless pit, that dark wood slipping below the lip of the grave forever.

Anor Woodruff, Rockford's Candy Man

Kathi Kresol

"And there are never really endings, happy or otherwise. Things keep going on, they overlap and blur, your story is part of your sister's story is part of many other stories, and there is no telling where any of them may lead."

—Erin Morgenstern, *The Night Circus*

May 24, 1888. "At 8 o'clock yesterday afternoon the death Angel's wings darkened the door of the humble cottage of Anor Woodruff, the old candy man, and all alone, his life help mate absent from his bedside, peacefully, quietly, willingly the tired spirit passed to eternal rest."

This quote ended the story of an old man; a man named Anor Woodruff. He was well known for his ever-ready smile and made famous for the old fashioned molasses candy that "won for him a warm place in hundreds of young hearts."

His story began in Connecticut on October 9, 1797, when Anor was born to his parents. When he was still a child, Anor met Eliza. They lived on adjoining farms. She was 12-years-old and Anor would say later that he loved her from first sight. He waited until he was 20 to ask her father for her hand in marriage. They were married on January 28, 1819 in Marlboro, Massachusetts.

The couple first settled in Hudson, New York where they opened a tavern and ran it for 18 years. They moved to Rockford, Illinois in 1839. At the time, Rockford had a population of 500. Anor and Eliza built a house on South Church Street. They opened a boarding house there to accommodate the men employed in building a dam across the Rock River.

This was about the time that Anor started to make his own molasses candy. He would become famous for this and continued to thrill children with it for over fifty years. He made it right in the kitchen of his boarding house.

Anor earned the nickname of Candy Man. His wife and he would also earn another title. They had been married for 67 years. They were the longest living couple during their time. Anor would tell anyone who would listen that he fell in love with Eliza when he first laid eyes on her when she was 12-years-old and he would love her until the day he died.

Anor didn't always have it easy, but no matter what life brought his way, he just accepted it as "what happens sometimes." He never became bitter or disillusioned. He thought of each day as a celebration to share with his wife, his family, and his community. When he died, people wrote in about Rockford's Candy Man.

One young lady, Jane Dale wrote, "Woodruff's Molasses Candy is a common memory. To think of him now is to recall all the boys and girls that we knew. It brings us back to Kent Creek, where we waded and the hungry minnows nibbled at our feet. It calls to mind the stone quarry and the big red bull, that always chased us out of the meadow back of it. We cannot think of Anor without remembering the county fair, when it was, to us, the greatest event on earth. Was not one of the chief features of that marvelous attraction Woodruff's molasses candy? We forget, when we think of him that he didn't belong to us alone. He was so identified with our childhood that it is difficult to remember that he belonged to generations of school boy and girls before us—generations since. Yet, for nearly fifty years each era of Rockford school children owned him."

The Woodruffs were one of the founding families of Rockford, and Anor Woodruff was one man among many who made his way here to build a living for his family. He could have settled anywhere, but he saw something in the little village along the Rock River. Anor saw someplace where he could make a difference, so he set down roots and became a piece of the wonderful tapestry of Rockford's past.

Works Cited

"Married sixty-nine years," *Daily Register* (Rockford) 24 May 1888.

"The old candy man," *Daily Register* (Rockford) 6 June 1888.

"Four score and eleven," *Daily Gazette* (Rockford) 24 May 1888.

DID THE ZODIAC KILLER ONCE WALK AMONG US?

BRANDON REID

Working as an editor at a weekly newspaper in Rockford, Ill., is a little like being a lightning rod in the middle of a highly-charged storm of insanity. An economically depressed, largely undereducated, highly crime-ridden community led by a mostly self-interested and corrupt political elite can offer many interesting and compelling stories. I've heard many of them, written about many of them, and also have been a part in uncovering many of them for *The Rock River Times*. The following ranks among the most bizarre news encounters I have experienced.

In 2004, a man entered our small office on North Church Street in downtown Rockford. He asked to speak with an editor. I approached him, shook his hand, and introduced myself. He asked if there were a more private place to meet in our office. I told him, "No, this is a small office, and unfortunately, this is as private as it gets."

The man began to speak, and I could tell immediately by the creases on his face and the tears in his eyes that what he was about to tell me was very difficult for him.

After listening to this man's story—which will remain unrepeated here in an attempt to protect the identities of those involved—we ran a series of articles in the newspaper about his experiences.

Many months after the series appeared in the newspaper, I received an envelope in the mail with no return address. The Post Office stamp was Palatine, Ill. Considering all mail sent from Rockford at the time was being sent through Palatine, I concluded the letter was likely sent from Rockford.

The letter appeared in a plain white envelope with no return address, one stamp, the postmark of "Palatine IL 600 11 MAR 2006PM 4 T," and a neatly-written address in cursive and in black ink. The writing appeared to be lined up with a ruler because the descenders were cut off.

The handwriting on the single sheet of paper inside the envelope was just as neat. The letter read as follows:

"On this, you'll have to make your own case! There's a remote possibility that [one of the individuals in the series of articles] may have been mixed up with the elusive Zodiac Killer down in Riverside California. This artist drawing from the RPD (Riverside Police Department) appears to resemble him."

Following the text of the letter was a lineup of images that included a police sketch of the Zodiac killer, a mugshot photo clipped from our newspaper of the individual from the series of articles, followed by another police sketch of the Zodiac Killer. The images were perfectly lined up, three across, centered on the page. Another police sketch of the Zodiac Killer was lined up in the center of those three pictures, underneath the picture of the individual from our series of articles. Each image had been copied and reduced to the exact same size, and the package of four photos was outlined in perfectly straight lines with thick, black marker.

Following the lineup of photos, the person who sent the letter included the following line, which was typed out on the page and was originally from a Zodiac Killer letter sent to newspapers in California:

"I. I look like the description passed out only when I do my thing, the rest of the time I look entirely different. I shall not tell you what my descise consist of when I kill."

The misspelled word ("descise" instead of "disguise") was also misspelled in the original letter from Zodiac.

Centered underneath that line of text were nearly 2-inches of text copied from our newspaper and centered on the page. Again, in attempts to be as vague as possible to conceal the identity of those involved in the series of articles, this block of text detailed the past residences by year of the individual from our series of articles.

Being a Midwesterner and having little knowledge of the Zodiac Killer at the time, I began to do some research. The identity of the Zodiac Killer remains one of the country's most notorious crime mysteries. The serial killer was the focus of the 2007 movie *Zodiac*, directed by David Fincher and starring Jake Gyllenhaal, Mark Ruffalo, Anthony Edwards, and Robert Downey Jr. Although the critically-acclaimed film drew national attention to the case, the movie was released well more than a year after the letter about the

Zodiac was sent to our newspaper, meaning the letter to our newspaper was written before the Zodiac Killer was in the national consciousness.

For those who have not seen the movie and are unaware of the story of the Zodiac Killer, the Zodiac Killer was a serial killer who operated in northern California from at least the late 1960s to at least the early 1970s. These dates are based on confirmed Zodiac murders. However, some followers of the case have speculated that other documents and crimes committed prior to the 1960s and after the 1970s may be attributed to the Zodiac.

What is known is that the Zodiac murdered victims in the California towns of Benicia, Vallejo, Lake Berryessa and San Francisco between December 1968 and October 1969. Four men and three women, ages 16-29, were targeted in the killings.

The Zodiac was particularly notorious for his taunting of investigators through a series of letters sent to Bay Area newspapers. The letters included four cryptograms, or ciphers. You can read the letters and ciphers, and find other Zodiac information, theories and discussions, online at www.zodiackiller.com.

Only one of the Zodiac's ciphers has ever been solved. On August 1, 1969, the *Vallejo Times-Chronicle*, the *San Francisco Examiner*, and the *San Francisco Chronicle* all received nearly identical letters from the Zodiac. In the letters, the Zodiac took credit for the series of murders. He proved his identity as the true Zodiac by providing details of the crimes only the killer would have known, such as what the victims were wearing, how their bodies were positioned when they were killed, and what brand of ammunition was used. The only signature on the letters was the same signature used on all Zodiac communication, a symbol resembling gun cross hairs — a circle with a cross through it.

Included with each of the three letters, the Zodiac sent one part of a three-part cipher. With the threat of going on a killing spree if the newspapers did not comply, the Zodiac Killer ordered all three publications to publish the ciphers on their front pages. All three newspapers did publish the ciphers, and the code was cracked a little more than a week later by David and Betty Harden of Salinas,

California.

The decoded cipher, with original misspellings, read as follows:

"I LIKE KILLING PEOPLE BECAUSE IT IS SO MUCH FUN IT IS MORE FUN THAN KILLING WILD GAME IN THE FORREST BECAUSE MAN IS THE MOST DANGERTUE ANAMAL OF ALL TO KILL SOMETHING GIVES ME THE MOST THRILLING EXPERENCE IT IS EVEN BETTER THAN GETTING YOUR ROCKS OFF WITH A GIRL THE BEST PART OF IT IS THAE WHEN I DIE I WILL BE REBORN IN PARADICE AND ALL THE I HAVE KILLED WILL BECOME MY SLAVES I WILL NOT GIVE YOU MY NAME BECAUSE YOU WILL TRY TO SLOI DOWN OR ATOP MY COLLECTING OF SLAVES FOR MY AFTERLIFE EBEORIETEMETHHPITI."

Many Zodiac suspects have been named by law enforcement and amateur investigators over the years, but no conclusive evidence has ever been found. The case was marked inactive by the San Francisco Police Department in 2004, but was re-opened prior to March 2007. The case remains open in Vallejo, Napa County, and Solano County. An open case file on the Zodiac murders has been held by the California Department of Justice since 1969.

While it is, as the author of the letter to our newspaper suggested, a "remote possibility" that the individual in our series was involved with the Zodiac murders, a number of interesting similarities exist between the Zodiac and the individual from our series. First, the mugshot from our newspaper of the individual from our series greatly resembled police sketches of the Zodiac Killer. Second, lining up this individual's previous places of residence, the person from our series clearly could have been in close proximity to each of the alleged Zodiac killings. Third, the individual from our series would have matched the same age, height, and weight description of the Zodiac Killer.

Beyond these similarities, and some other details that cannot be shared here to protect the identity of this individual, there is little to suggest this individual was the Zodiac Killer. What continues to be intriguing, however, even years after the letter was received by our newspaper, is the condition in which the anonymous letter was sent. Someone took great care and time to prepare the letter anonymously. Why was it anonymous? Does the person who sent the letter to our newspaper know more about the case? Or was that person just afraid of sounding like a wacko? Most wackos I have dealt with in my years as a journalist are not afraid to share their identities while providing news tips. Also, how many people in the Rockford area at the time—prior to the release of the *Zodiac* movie—really knew enough about Zodiac to make the connection between a mugshot in a weekly newspaper in Rockford, Ill., and police sketches of the Zodiac done in the 1960s and 1970s in California? Prior to receiving this letter, I would have said no one.

The anonymous letter to our newspaper remains just one more mystery in a much grander mystery—one marked by murder, violence, and tragedy. As long as the mystery of the Zodiac Killer remains unsolved, we can always wonder whether the Zodiac Killer may have once walked among us in the city of Rockford.

WILD WINDS

NICOLE C. LINDSAY

It is true what they say—it sounded like a freight train coming straight at us. The sound woke my husband and me around 4:30am on the morning of Saturday July 5, 2003. Our condominium, located just off Alpine and East State Street, occupied the second and third floors. As I stood in our living room, I felt water dripping onto my forehead. I watched the trees bend eastward and the rain come down sideways outside our living room's sliding glass door while water rushed in. I was convinced that it must have been a tornado and that we should either get in the bathtub or run to the basement of the building.

Then, as quickly as it began, it was all over. The building was still standing, the roof was still attached, and we discovered that the water was coming from the windows in our loft. It had been raining so hard that leaks had been exposed. I could see trees snapped in half outside in the darkness, debris littered all over the tennis court, and I was left wondering what had just happened.

Needless to say, I had trouble going back to sleep. On the television a little bit later, the speculation was that it had not been a tornado, but straight-line winds at around eighty to one hundred miles per hour. The more technical term was a "*derecho*," but I had never heard of such a thing. I noticed while flipping through the channels that several, including the local CBS affiliate WIFR Channel 23, were not coming in. A call to my parents, who lived next door to the television stationed, confirmed why. The station's transmission tower had toppled over like it was made out of Legos. I imagined what that must have sounded like to those who were in the television station at the time.

My parents, my brother and sister, and my grandparents who were visiting from out of town had heard the same freight train noise and had taken shelter in the basement during the storm. They emerged to find the red and white transmission tower collapsed in the field to the east. If it had collapsed to the south, their house would most likely have been hit and severely damaged. There were also several other houses nearby which could have been affected as well.

My husband and I headed over to my parents' house Saturday morning to help with the cleanup in their yard and to get a look at the tower. On the drive over, we saw hundreds of trees snapped in half and debris everywhere. Downed power lines and power outages could also be seen. The drive took a bit longer due to stoplights not working. In short, the city looked like a disaster zone. We knew that in some cases, it would take months to repair some of the damage. When we arrived at my parents' house, we saw that the wood fence around their pool, along with many of the trees in their yard (including a massive one in the front yard), had been knocked down or damaged. But by far the most startling sight was the tower lying in the grassy field to the east of the television station. It was no longer a tower of over seven hundred feet, but instead a twisted mess of metal on the ground tangled with the cables that had previously held it in place.

As we started the cleanup of my parents' yard, we started to notice a steady stream of cars on Steverlund Drive. At the time, my parents' house was the only one on the street and it was situated at the end of a cul-de-sac. Never had this street seen so much traffic. The only time they saw traffic was either when someone came to see them, or someone had made a wrong turn and needed to turn around. Yet, car after car began stopping in the cul-de-sac as people got out to take a look and, in many cases, take pictures of the collapsed tower. Many asked us what had happened and what the storm sounded like. Eventually, the stream of cars became so numerous that the Rockford Police Department showed up and informed us that a car and policeman would be stationed at the end of the cul-de-sac to keep people from traipsing through the field or my parents' yard and getting too close to the collapsed tower. The metal pieces and cables could be quite dangerous if they were to shift or snap.

The other television stations reported that Channel 23 would be off the air for a couple of days until they could establish a connection to those with cable. A permanent fix, however, would take much longer, probably months.

Over the next few days, the whole city worked on cleaning up the mess from the storm. Several area parks and golf courses had to close in order to clean up the downed trees and debris. Many of the trees were decades old and had been snapped in half or uprooted like they were twigs. As the cleanup continued at my parents' house, so too did the steady stream of people who wanted to see the damage to the tower. Since they couldn't turn into the station's parking lot, they drove onto the street where my parents' house was located. Friends came over to the house to take a look at the damage, which could easily be seen by standing in my parents' front yard or driveway. Many commented on how lucky they were that their house was fine and that nobody was hurt or even killed by the tower collapse. We joked that if we started charging admission to see the tower, we would make a fortune. We also talked about setting up a beverage stand to bring in some extra cash.

Over the next four months, the process of cleaning up the pieces of the collapsed tower and installing a new one took place. First, the red and white metal pieces lying in the field were hauled away piece by piece, along with the broken cables. The process of installing the new tower was much more fascinating.

Living by television stations since I was ten years old, first in a house by the ABC affiliate WTVO Channel 17 and then WIFR Channel 23, I had seen men on the towers and cables many times before checking for what I assumed were safety reasons and sometimes even painting them. I would sit on the deck and look up at the blue sky as the men worked. It always amazed me how a man got smaller and smaller the higher he climbed until you almost couldn't see him anymore when he neared the top. I marveled at what it must be like to look down from their point of view. I remember thinking maybe they can see me too and sometimes I would wave. When they were at lower altitudes some of them did wave back. It reminded me of the famous 1932 black and white picture *Lunch atop a Skyscraper*, which showed a group of men eating during construction of the RCA Building (now the GE Building) in New York City.

I periodically stopped by my parents' house to watch the new tower being erected and found it just as fascinating and also frightening in a way. Gradually, the red and white tower grew taller and taller and new cables and anchors were put in place. The tower was installed in sections. The men would start on the ground attaching what I assumed were various harnesses and safety devices to themselves and then they would become tiny specks the higher they went. At times, they almost looked like birds in the sky to me. I wondered if the tower and cables would be stronger than before and if they would withstand another storm. So far, they have. I also wondered why the other television towers in the area did not collapse, especially since three of them are so close together.

As the rebuilding process continued, others were as intrigued as I was and continued to drive down the street, park in the cul-de-sac, and watch the work progress. There was no longer a need for a policeman to be stationed there, but the people kept coming and taking pictures. They would peer up into the sky with their hands shielding their eyes from the sun and point to the men as they worked. By the middle of November, the station had a brand new tower and was back on the air.

It is now ten years later and my grandpa, as well as both of my parents, have passed away. The house is no longer in my family's possession, but people still talk about the storm and what happened when my parents lived there. It's a reminder of the power of Mother Nature, but also the resiliency of this city and those who call it home.

TAMING NUCLEAR
POWER IN BYRON

STANLEY CAMPBELL

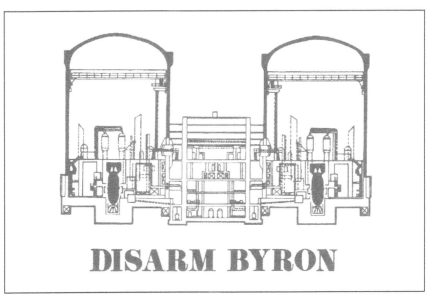

DISARM BYRON

Postcard designed by Stanley Campbell opposing the Byron
Nuclear Generating Station

Betty Johnson, Jane Whicher, and Stanley Campbell | Photo
by a friend of Stanley Campbell, 1983

In the mid-1970s, I thought nuclear power was safe, clean, and would be so cheap you wouldn't even need to meter it. That was the promise of Eisenhower's sales campaign "Atoms for Peace." In 1977, however, a friend of mine got arrested at the Seabrook Nuclear Power Plant in New Hampshire while trying to scale a fence to occupy the construction site. I raised money to bail him out. At the time, there were news reports about "Vietnam War protesters searching for a cause." I was an activist and knew we didn't have to search for causes—there were plenty.

Using the local public library, I found authors John Goffman and Rosalie Bertel. I also connected with Chicago Citizens Against Nuclear Power (CANP). They'd sponsored a demonstration at the Morris, Illinois, nuclear waste dump. In the summer of 1979, I joined three Rockfordians going to that protest. We heard speakers and saw a balloon release showing which way the radiation would blow. On the drive back, the four of us (Peter Reilly, Mark Pemble, Laurie Searles, and myself) thought up the name Sinnissippi Alliance for the Environment (acronym SAFE). We'd just formed our anti-nuclear power group.

There were few national organizations opposing nuclear power. One of them was the Mobilization For Survival (The MOBE), which raised support for human needs and also opposed nuclear weapons and foreign wars. SAFE joined The MOBE in 1980, and sent representatives from Rockford to national conventions until 1992.

SAFE brought in speakers from Northern Illinois University. Two professors, Dr. Bruce Von Zellen and Dr. Axel Meyers, had already founded an organization two years before called DeKalb Area Alliance for Responsible Energy, DAARE. In fact, it was this organization that sent some of their members to the Seabrook Nuclear Power Plant, including my friend, Court Dorsey (he sang in the musical group *Bright Morningstar*).

By organizing public programs and leafleting the downtown area, SAFE began to attract more supporters, including environmentalists and peace activists. SAFE also sponsored a Hiroshima commemoration, usually the Sunday nearest August 6-9

(Nagasaki was nuked three days later in 1945). SAFE's first memorial in 1980 met at an outdoor rally in Beattie Park with speakers and musicians. We tried to float candles in the Rock River, in a manner similar to Hiroshima commemorations, but they quickly disappeared downstream.

Betty Johnson (a member of Westminster Presbyterian) just returned from Japan with an actual floating lantern. In 1981, Betty showed us how to construct lanterns using a Styrofoam base and homemade rice paper. Children were invited to draw peace signs on the paper. By the next year we moved across the river and hosted a potluck picnic with the program, south of the Symbol statue. By the fifth year, though, we gave up trying to float the candles in the Rock River and had people hold them as twilight came.

Our speakers included Sam Day from *Progressive Magazine* in Madison, Wisconsin, representatives from the *Bulletin for Atomic Scientists*, and local musicians. We still try to host a program every year sponsored by Rockford Peace and Justice Action Committee and Rockford Urban Ministries.

In March 1983, the Three-Mile Island nuclear accident occurred at Harrisburg, Pennsylvania. We immediately leafleted the downtown area, put out press releases, and hosted a program at the Friends House at 623 N. Avon Street. That was the home of Rock Valley Friends Meeting (Quakers). Over 90 people crowded into that small space! SAFE gained more supporters and a few activists.

The focus of our attention was slowly drawn to the Byron Nuclear Power Plant, which was just under construction 17 miles downwind from Rockford, along the Rock River. Betty Johnson, as a representative of the League of Women Voters, had opposed it since the utility's initial planning. She was planning on "intervening" against the operating license for the power plant. We learned from Betty that the laws of atomic power included a chance for citizens to legally oppose the construction or operation of a power plant. By 1980, Betty and the local League of Women Voters had already hired an attorney to represent their concerns before the Atomic Safety and Licensing Board (ASLB) of the Nuclear Regulatory Commission (NRC).

Meanwhile, SAFE sponsored a large demonstration on Saturday, May 24, 1983. We planned a rally in Rockford and one in DeKalb that would send people to the Byron Nuclear Power Plant. As a gesture of goodwill, we met with the publicist for Commonwealth Edison to work out demonstration logistics. Representing SAFE was Nancy Rust, Beth Galbraith (wife of a United Methodist minister), and myself. Right away we were accused of being "communists" and "out to destroy the electric grid of the America."

So we met with the Sheriff of Ogle County. He suggested ComEd might let us use their parking lot in front of the power plant instead of us just standing in the middle of the road. He phoned the utility and said that for the safety of all concerned, we should be allowed onto ComEd's property. The demonstration attracted over 400 people to the Byron plant. At the time, we were disappointed at the small turnout, but since then I've learned 400 was an impressive number.

Betty Johnson came to a SAFE meeting (about 1982) and suggested that SAFE and DAARE "intervene" against the operating license of Byron. SAFE was split—do we "work within the system" or just stand outside with a sign? After much discussion we decided to intervene. Bruce Von Zellen contacted Mary Sinclair of Midland, Michigan, and asked if DAARE/SAFE could use 'contentions' that their group had developed against the Midland Nuclear Power Plant (another Westinghouse nuke). We filed and were accepted as legal interveners. I found a public interest law firm in Chicago called Business and Professionals in the Public Interest (BPI) that was opposed to ComEd's rate hikes, and they assigned a lovely young attorney, Jane Whicher, to represent DAARE/SAFE before the Atomic Safety and Licensing Board (ASLB).

DAARE/SAFE joined the illustrious world of nuclear interveners, trained and supported by the Nuclear Information and Resource Service (NIRS) in Washington DC.

The first hearings were delaying tactics and the League grew disenchanted with the high cost of their attorney, so they agreed to "hiring" Jane Whicher as their representative and combine our three groups' contentions. Hearings started in 1983 and went for four months before three judges, during which time I lost my job at Care-A-Van (a transportation service for elderly and handicapped) where I'd been their dispatcher.

During the trials, Jane would direct us in the minutiae of taking care of the witnesses, filing paperwork, making copies, and running out for sandwiches. Local Attorney Brian Savage helped by cross-examining Com Ed's witnesses about their evacuation plans. Brian was able to solicit from the sheriff that volunteers and staff would probably evacuate along with their families instead of stay and direct traffic.

Volunteer Diane Chavez did an amazing job of cross-examining Westinghouse engineers about their problems with steam generators. I cross-examined ComEd's witness on the probability of an accident and established that if the plant was built incorrectly, something could go wrong, even with all the "redundancy."

Jane Whicher focused on faulty construction, and had SAFE solicit construction workers who had information about problems. We received eight serious complaints, three of which were written up and presented as evidence of malfeasance. With help from the Government Accountability Project (GAP), SAFE provided some modicum of protection for these whistle-blowers.

ComEd was represented by the law firm of Isham, Lincoln, and Beale (that's the famous Todd Lincoln, the president's son). Three or four of their attorneys showed up in Rockford with a gaggle of secretaries and paralegals. Their witnesses were from the nuclear industry. We felt outgunned and overwhelmed and that it was a lost cause. We waited six months for the decision.

On Friday, January 13, 1984, while working at the City of Rockford's Human Services Department, I received a phone call from a TV station. They wanted my response to the ruling. I asked what the ruling had been, and they said the license was denied. What a day! I fielded questions and called Betty Johnson and the rest of the gang. *Rockford Register Star* reporter Eileen Peterson, who'd covered the hearings, was so flustered she could barely type.

That evening, Betty Johnson and I shared a victory hug and danced on her frozen front porch.

ComEd's attorneys' defense hadn't worked. While DAARE/SAFE raised serious concerns before the three judges about the quality of construction, Isham, Lincoln, and Beale's defense was "Hey, this is ComEd... they've built 13 reactors across Northern Illinois. Who ya gonna trust?" As one of the judges later admitted, we'd established a record that the ASLB could not ignore. They had to deny the license.

A year later, during the re-hearing, ComEd claimed they'd reinspected every one of the specific concerns that the interveners had raised. Even though SAFE received further complaints, we were not allowed to present them, and ComEd finally got its license to operate late in 1985. It took them almost another year to actually bring the plant online.

The hearing produced several good results. The "domino theory" didn't happen in Southeast Asia, but it worked with nukes: five utilities threw in the towel and stopped construction (probably figuring if ComEd couldn't win...), one was the Midland Nuclear Plant—it was built over a swamp and they never could lay a cement foundation. BPI used much of the information gleaned from our hearings to defeat Com Ed's future rate hike requests ("You expect the ratepayers to cover your malfeasance?!").

Isham, Lincoln & Beale went bankrupt, Jane Whicher left BPI to defend women's rights with the American Civil Liberties Union, and as ComEd officials constantly remind me, the plant is one of the safest operating nukes in the country.

INTERVIEW WITH
JESUS CORREA VII

MICHAEL KLEEN

Jesus A. Correa VII | Photo by Brian Milo

Jesus Abraham Correa VII was born and raised in Rockford, Illinois. He has been saying Yes to the No-no's since 1979 and he intends to do so until his untimely death. A self-made, self-taught man, Jesus has been creating in the fields of music, visual art, literature, and stand-up comedy for the past fifteen years.

As a musician, Mr. Correa has run the gamut from angry violent punk rock to the sweet folky twee tunes about love and Jell-O and iced cream. He currently performs with the much loved and universally respected King of the Demons outfit, as well as his own personal one man pet project called *los osos voladores*.

Jesus Correa's visual art has come to be known for its detailed black ink illustration work as well as the kinetic sculptures and hand knitted masks and puppets. His work has appeared in numerous shows beginning in 2003 in an old warehouse on Rockford's dwindling north side, and culminating in travelling to Miami and New York to show with other local artists in the prestigious Fountain Art Fair. Correa has had a total of six solo gallery shows in the course of his fine art career and is currently working on his seventh as well as a long awaited comic book.

If that wasn't enough, Mr. Correa has been a stand-up comedian, and was the Green Party nominee for Mayor of Rockford in 2009. He has compiled a few of his short story writings and intends to release it over the course of the year as *Date Night: Tales to Set the Mood for Young Lovers*.

Please tell us a little about your background. In what neighborhood of Rockford did you grow up? Where did you go to high school? College?

I grew up mostly in a little trailer park on South Main St. across the road from where the Klehm Arboretum now resides. I was a lonely little boy and kept to myself quite a bit. I was in the Gifted Program from the second grade until I eventually dropped out in my junior year due to family issues and bad bouts with insomnia. I dropped out of Auburn and tried going back a few times to Guilford, but I just couldn't take it seriously, it was very unchallenging going to the plain old Rockford Public Schooling curriculum, so I stopped going to Guilford as well.

I eventually got my G.E.D. and got a free college course because I had done so well. I took a Political Science course at Rock Valley College. I remember this being soon after 9/11 because the "Professor" and I would butt heads about certain current event topics. He thought I was a conspiracy nut, and I thought he was an asshole. I am fairly close to getting my associates but it is not anything I feel compelled to do any time soon.

You have explored many artistic mediums over the years, from music, to art, and spoken word. What is your favorite creative medium, and why?

It depends on the time of the year and what is going on in my life. I enjoy the solitude of doing my illustrations or paintings, or what have you, but I really, really enjoy the immediacy of a live crowd. Live music crowd is fantastic, but a live comedy crowd is fantastically scary, which is great. You know when you have lost a comedy crowd, and I enjoy fighint my way out of corners, and I even have learned to enjoy bombing. So as far as creation, I enjoy making visual art more, but as far as actual feedback of the finished product, I would much rather be performing in a bar than feeling very stuffy and anxious at an art opening.

What do you like most about being an artist in Rockford? What do you like least?

I like that I can just do whatever the hell I want, but I think I just sort of did that on my own. If you want to try and make a go of it here in Rockford as a creative type, you are going to have to understand that no one is going to really hold your hand, because there is no real defined way to go about doing things around here. I have always thought of this town as a blank slate, no one has really done anything exceptional with it, so if you were really a visionary, you could really mold the hell out of this place, because it is a pretty nondescript town. As far as what I like least about being a Rockford artist, I don't like that more people do not recognize my genius, and I don't like how little of their money they are willing to give to me. Give me your money Rockford.

What was your most memorable performance?

I have been performing for fifteen years, so there are a lot of things that come to mind. The one that sticks out in my head right now happened during my friend Jack Kooistra's band Alpha Drops show. I just played a bit part in the show, but I was very vested in my role. So Jack and I had it worked out that I would come onstage during his set, just sort of invite myself up after he called me out in the crowd. So I get onstage and I start insulting his music, saying stuff like, "I listen to real music, I listen to The Beatles, I listen to Led Zeppelin..." etc. and just insulting his singing voice, and I am just having fun, and I remember the crowd getting a bit worked up.

Then out of nowhere this lady grabs me and starts yelling at me, and I just keep going, but I am sort of freaked out that this older woman is this upset with me, but sort of loving that this old lady is upset with me. Jack and I had the whole thing scripted out and worked, but he didn't tell me he had planted his mother to get upset with me. So, I think I am getting over on the crowd, but I am the one who got got. It was fun. I like pissing people off.

In 2002 you suffered severe burns during a musical performance. What happened, and how did you come back from the accident? How did the accident and your recovery add uniqueness to your art?

Right, I burned myself onstage at Mary's Place while performing with my punk band Popeye Jonesin'. During a song about dragons we were going to light a stuffed bird on fire, but they said no, so what I did was take the rubbing alcohol meant for the bird and I pour it on myself during the Dragonslayer song and I light it on fire as I scream "BURN!!!" So, the fire goes out, I want more fire, I pour on more rubbing alcohol, light that sumbitch up...and it just sort of won't go out, blah blah blah, I am standing naked in the middle of Mary's Place, skin dangling from all over me...

I go home, take a shower...start going into shock... go to the E.R. at Swedes... get a helicopter ride to Loyola in Chicago... two weeks in the burn unit... a few months of physical therapy to learn to use my hands again. Just learning to use my hands again was a miracle to me, it was amazing, and I just felt compelled to make things. I thought I was going to die, and I did not, and that made me want to live my life a little bit better and bigger. It was like putting a big beautiful gun to my head.

Tell us a little about your musical tastes and the bands you have performed in over the years. Is there a particular sound to which you're drawn?

My taste in music is all over the place, as are the musical styles I have messed with. I am seriously all over the place, and every project feels like starting all over again, not one of them sounds anything like the last one. My first band was a jazzy ska band, then onto a sort of punk-rap-wrestling band, I did a recording rap project for a few years, then experimental electronic music, a band called lightning thunder fox which consisted of myself and two girls, it was what I guess they would call twee music.

Nowadays I perform with two outfits. One is a solo project called *los osos voladores*. It's electronic folk music, I use samples and drum machines and keyboards and weird gizmos, and that is very loose and I just sort of experiment and try things out with that outfit.

The other band is King of the Demons which is a five piece band that someone told me would be the ideal band to perform at a bar brawl in a motion picture. King of the Demons started out as me and my friend Jon Miller switching some of my tunes over into a more country and western feel. It has grown to cover all sorts of musical genres, and we keep growing and experimenting, and it is probably the best band I have had the chance to perform with. It feels very exciting, and it feels like rock n' roll should feel, alive and dangerous.

How has the Rockford art scene changed over the past 15-20 years? Do you think the city government helps or hinders local artists?

I guess the main thing I have noticed as far as change is that a lot of the good local artists have left, and everyone seems to want to talk about art all the time around here, but I don't see that many people actually producing. I don't think the city government really needs to have that much to do with local artists. I know they haven't done a damned thing for me, and I am just fine with that. An artist working with the government just sort of feels wrong to me, but that is just my opinion.

What do you think local businessmen, average citizens, and other artists can do to grow Rockford's art scene? Has the First Friday event downtown successfully drawn more attention to local artists?

Local businessmen can give me their money and their real estate. Average citizens can come out to the shows I will put on with the local businessman's money. Other artists can just keep on working, and creating, and putting themselves out there for the average citizen to ignore or ridicule. I'd rather be ridiculed than ignored any old day. The First Friday event has given certain people in this town an opportunity to make bland posters and pat themselves on the backs. I have never had anything to do with the event or the Element besides when I happen to be playing a show at one of the venues on one of their posters. I have nothing to do with them, and they have nothing to do with me, and that is just fine with me.

Why did you decide to run for Mayor of Rockford in 2009? Why did you choose to run as a Green Party candidate? Was it difficult to get on the ballot?

I had talked jokingly about running for mayor for years. I was very disappointed with my local Government and I had nothing better to do. I originally was running as a Democrat, but I lost my original paperwork, which I took as a sign that I should just get out of the race. Fast forward a bit and I am reading a newspaper, and they mention the local Deocratic candidates, and there is my name followed by the sentiment..."Who the hell is this guy? Our party is doomed."

So I looked in to some things, it was late in the race, and I read that I could get on the ballot with a lot less signatures if I ran as a Green Party Candidate, and I would be running unopposed, and I was more in tune with the Green Party values than I was with the Democratic Party. It was a lot easier to get on the ballot than I thought. I thought for sure I would be booted off the ballot. I filed my own paperwork, and haphazardly ran my own campaign.

How did your friends and family react when you told them you were running for mayor?

Kind of hard to say. No one got on board enough to actually help me in the whole planning out a platform or anything, I had some discussions with friends and would try and slip in their points during debates when I could. My friend Javier Jiminez of Saturated Threads printed up some shirts and Jesus For Mayor yard signs with my face on them. I think they might be the nicest yard signs I have ever seen.

What did you think of your opponents? If you hadn't been in the race, who would you have voted for, and why?

I liked John Harmon, and I would have voted for him had I not voted for myself. The other two were very much politicians, not human, and I didn't get to know them very well. All their answers seemed very empty and I would just sit there during the debates sometimes at how some people can string so many words together and still make no sense. Jon Harmon just made the most sense to me, and he didn't make my skin crawl as a human being.

What did you learn about Rockford politics during that election?

I learned that we can be just as sleazy and untruthful and disearnest here as they are in the big cities. I learned that the system is sort of rigged and everything is run by money.

Do you think Rockford has improved since the election in 2009? If not, what is holding us back and how can we move forward?

Not particularly, nope. What is holding us back is that we as a people are apathetic and we do not elect people who could actually change things around here. People do not vote in local elections. Only twenty percent of folks who were eligible to vote in 2009 voted. So you get people just sliding on in there, and everything is stagnant or rotting. I am getting less and less Rockford Gung-ho. We don't deserve better than this, because we don't work for or envision better than this. I wish Jon Anderson were mayor. I think that man is a genius and I would be proud to have someone like that as my mayor.

FOOTPRINTS

KATHI KRESOL

Friends and relatives of slain Kimberley McMillan pay last respects

Register-Republic photo

"There is no footprint too small to leave an imprint on this world."
—Author unknown

It was a bright summer day—a hot one from all those who spoke of it later, and many did speak of it. Not that I was there. Not that day anyway. I lived close by and had been to the park, but I wasn't there on that day.

It was 1971. I was eight-years-old. I don't remember that specific day, or any specific day from that summer. The days all blended into one another. I lived in my own head to hide from all the fighting and yelling, and all the promises that there would be no divorce and that mommy and daddy loved each other and sometimes people fought. The slamming doors. The dinner plates thrown and smashed. The days my mother wouldn't leave her room, and the days my father didn't come home. I hid from all of these things.

Until that day. At first, I didn't know what happened. It's hard to understand such adult things as an eight-year-old. I just knew that things changed after that day. We weren't allowed to walk to the store alone anymore. We weren't allowed to go anywhere alone for a while. When we would ask why, the grownups would turn their eyes quickly away and grow quiet. They would stand together in groups outside and when one of us kids approached they would shush each other and send us away. I didn't know what really happened until years later.

There were 30 people or so in the park that August day, though some reports said it was closer to 60. It was a good park in a nice area. A lot of older people and young families with little children lived all around the park. Parents felt safe letting their children play there. The kids all went together and stayed until after dark most summer nights.

Kimberley McMillian had only lived in the neighborhood a couple of weeks. Her mother had remarried and Kimberley's step-father, Eldon Hardcastle, moved the family from Knoxville, Tennessee to Rockford somewhere around 1965. They bought the house on Sunset Avenue just nine weeks before. Kimberley and her brother Charles had spent their summer with the father back in Tennessee. They had only been at the new house for two weeks.

They both had made new friends, and they gathered at the park most days to play.

Kimberley had taken her infant sister with her to the park on August 17 around noon so that her mother, Mrs. Hardcastle, could get another of Kimberley's siblings to take a nap. There were adults in the park. Some were even Park District employees, so Mrs. Hardcastle wasn't worried in the least for her children's safety. This fact made everything that was to follow so much more unbelievable.

The first inkling that something was wrong came when Kimberley was at the water fountain. All of a sudden, she fell to the ground. Everyone stepped back. She lay there bleeding. The reports taken that day all mention that her eyes were very big and looked to the adults, pleading for them to help her. She didn't speak any words. The only sounds were the moans that came from her bleeding mouth. People described how time seemed to stand still and everything became eerily silent. No one spoke or moved. Then a little voice rang out. Memories were jumbled, but the words, "little girl" and "hurt," and then louder, "Help!" were heard.

A family backing out of their driveway stopped their car and the mother, Mrs. Earlywine, ran to assist the little girl. She pushed her way through the crowd and knelt down beside Kimberley. Mrs. Earlywine reported later that the little girl was "bleeding profusely from her mouth and nose." She didn't see any obvious wounds on the girl's head and she couldn't attempt mouth-to-mouth resuscitation because Kimberley was bleeding too badly. A few minutes later, Mr. Earlywine arrived. He was able to assist Kimberley by removing a large blood clot that had formed in her mouth. Kimberley gasped a couple of times and then ...nothing.

As little Kimberley struggled for her last breath, her mother came upon the scene. Another child had run to Kimberley's house and told her that Kimberley was hurt. No one knew at that point what had happened to the little 10-year-old. I don't even want to imagine what the scene must have been like when Mrs. Hardcastle got to the park. People stepped aside to let her through the crowd.

She looked down at the body of her little girl and then overwhelmed by the sight she could not comprehend. She fainted.

The fire department arrived and whisked Kimberley into an ambulance and drove her to Rockford Memorial Hospital. She was dead on arrival. The hospital notified the police that they had dead child there. It was now around 1:28pm. Another call came from a "concerned citizen."

The late notification of the police would cause many problems for the investigation. The crime scene was horribly compromised by the crowd who flocked to see what happened. Police tried to question the people closest to where Kimberley collapsed, but it took a while to track them all down.

Winnebago County Coroner Collins Y. Sundberg performed an autopsy on the murdered little girl. He reported that she had been stabbed once between the shoulder blades with a knife that was at least a 6-inch double edged blade. It is horrible to think what a weapon like that could do to a small 10-year-old child.

Detective Ben Palmeri was put in charge of the case. "Apparently, she was going to the drinking fountain, or was drinking or had just left it when she was stabbed."

By Thursday, police had interviewed over 200 people who were in the park or the neighborhood that day. It seemed like each and every one of those 200 people saw something different. Some reported seeing a young man ride past Kimberley on a bicycle and punch out at her with an object wrapped in a towel.

Others reported seeing a young boy walk up to Kimberley as she was at the water fountain and bumped into her. That is when she fell to the ground.

On August 19, Police Chief Delbert Peterson told the *Morning Star* that police were looking for a black youth seen near the drinking fountain in Sunset Park where Kimberley was stabbed. "The young man was about 5 foot 2 inches, overweight, and wearing a gray polo shirt, black pants and tennis shoes."

The article went on to reveal that by Thursday, Park District supervisors were claiming that before the stabbing there were normally 60 children in the park on any given afternoon. On this Thursday, a few days after this horrible crime, the park was deserted.

On Friday, the paper mentioned that police had searched the park and surrounding neighborhood for the murder weapon, believed to be a knife. The searched had "turned up nothing."

Kimberley McMillian was buried on Friday, August 20, 1971. "Friday afternoon's hot summer breeze blew gently across the rolling Scandinavian Cemetery and rustled ever so slightly a bouquet of red roses which rested on the casket holding 10 year old Kimberley Kay McMillian," described the *Morning Star*.

50 close friends and relatives gathered to say goodbye to the once happy little girl. Some of these were the children she would have attended school with in a short few weeks. Her mother and step-father, who had been supported by their friends constantly since their ordeal began, were understandably grief-stricken. "We can't leave her here all alone," Mrs. Hardcastle cried as her husband attempted to lead her away at the end of the graveside service.

The whole family suffered terribly after Kimberley's death. Her brother Charles was particularly affected. He had almost uncontrollable fear about returning to the park or even to his home on Sunset Avenue. His step-father promised him they would move, and they did. According to later newspaper articles, the house stood empty for a long time.

Kimberley's murder was never solved. Eventually, Lewis Lemon Global Studies Academy was built in the place the park once stood. None of the original residents are left in the old neighborhood. The new playground was dedicated to Kimberley McMillian, but the children who play there now don't know who she was or why the park was named after her.

I often wonder when I drive past if Kimberley's murderer is still here. Does the "young man" (if that is indeed who killed her) still pass by the park? I don't have to wonder if he remembers her, I am certain of it, but I do wonder if there were others that he hurt. It seems that one who was so bold, bold enough to walk up to a little girl that was surrounded by dozens of eyewitnesses and stab her so brutally, would not be afraid to do it again.

So now, many years later, I know the details of the event that the adults in my life were so afraid to tell me. I now have children of my own, and I understand the horror that lives in the heart of a parent that knows Kimberley could have been one of his or her own children. The randomness of this act is what makes it so completely terrifying. It is also the fact that this crime was never solved. In an article written in 1972, the newspaper stated that the neighborhood had changed in the year since Kimberley was killed. "People want a solution that will permit a neighborhood, an entire city, to stop looking over its shoulder in fear."

There would, in fact, be no solution or logic to this crime, no apparent motive to the killing, no closure for her family, and no answers for the neighborhood.

Miles away from Kimberley's grave, the sound of children playing rings out in the park where she died. The blood stain is long gone, as is the water fountain that kept the terrible secret of what really happened that day. But Kimberley isn't forgotten, not by her family or any of the families that lived in Rockford during that time. Her death changed our lives and our community. The little girl whose footprints ran through that park on that summer day could have been mine or they could have been any one of ours.

The innocence that died that day was ours.

Works Cited

"Murder of girl, 10, 'senseless,'" *Register-Republic* (Rockford) Wednesday, August 18, 1971.

"10-year-old girl murdered," *Morning Star* (Rockford) Wednesday August 18, 1971.

"Obituary: McMillian, Kimberley K." *Register-Republic* (Rockford) Wednesday, August 18, 1971.

"God's Mystery: How could it happen?" *Morning Star* (Rockford) Saturday, August 21, 1971.

"Double edged knife killed McMillian girl" *Register-Republic* (Rockford) Monday, August 23, 1971.

"Girl, 10, slain in park a year ago today" *Morning Star* (Rockford) Thursday, August 18, 1972.

THE SKYDIVING
SANTA TRAGEDY

ERNIE FUHR

"**M**om, when are we going to see Santa?" 12-year-old Jimmy asked impatiently.

"As soon as your dad is ready to take us," his mom answered. "What's your hurry?"

"I don't want to wait in line behind all those crybabies." Jimmy was still a kid and expected gifts accordingly, but he was also at an awkward age and his parents had started to detect the obnoxiousness of an adolescent. Not that it mattered in the scheme of things; Santa's visit to North Towne Mall today would be a special occasion for children of all ages.

"Daddy! Jimmy called me a crybaby!" squealed his sister, Cindy. Sound travelled within the walls of the Johnson family's tiny Loves Park home.

"Shut up! I did not! Dad, are you ready?!"

Ray Johnson, a bleary-eyed ogre, emerged from the bathroom, freshly dressed and reeking of Old Spice. He was still exhausted from his third shift factory job and would've given anything to get out of today's family obligation. "Tell you what—if you *both* don't shut up, I'll tell Santa that you've been brats! And you won't get any presents this year! Neither of you!"

◆　　◆　　◆

Meanwhile, five miles away at the Greater Rockford Airport, Bill Fleming sat on the wing of an old crop duster as he made final adjustments to his Santa Claus costume, tucking his fake beard into his paratrooper jacket and lacing his boots. Nearby, his partner, Cornelius "Connie" O'Rourke, finished a smoke. Even after years of jumping out of planes, Connie still liked to have a cigarette to ease his nerves. He told friends that tobacco would kill him before skydiving ever did, and after 1,000 successful jumps, he was probably right.

Today, Connie played the role of "Santa's helper." The army uniform he had once worn proudly was replaced by a ridiculous green and red elf costume. Like any good elf, Connie had to think of the kids first, so he made sure that his puffy paratrooper pockets were loaded with candy.

"Ho-Ho-Ho!! How do I look?" Bill asked, stroking his fake Santa beard. "I'm gonna wear my helmet and then when I land, switch into my Santa hat."

Connie laughed. "We do what we gotta do, Bill! Even if we look like a couple dipshits in these costumes!"

"I hear ya, Connie. But we got a lot of kids counting on us today. So here's the plan: you land first. Get out of your gear and they'll pick you up in a golf cart. Then, when you get up to Santa's house, keep'em busy. They're supposed to have the kids behind the gates and all lined up. So, pass out your candy and ring your jingle bells and sing songs with'em and stuff. We'll be circling and once you get on the ground, I'll come in behind you. Let's give'em all a good show and when it's over I'll buy the first round."

"That's the spirit, Santa!" Connie chuckled. At 40-years-old, he was starting to feel a little old to be a skydiving elf, and his bum leg didn't help. Among the hundreds of children on the ground below, two of them were very special to Connie: his two little girls. The look in their eyes as they watched their daddy jump out of a plane made it all worthwhile to him, even if he was dressed up like an elf.

♦   ♦   ♦

As the Johnson family sat in traffic on the way to the mall, Sally Johnson made sure that her kids looked presentable. Cindy was easy to manage, but she no longer laid Jimmy's clothes out on the bed, like a little flat person. Ever since his classmates picked on him for plaid pants, Jimmy dressed himself. Sally laughed when she thought of how he'd disapprove of the dorky clothes he'd be getting this Christmas.

Ray lightened up when he looked at his kids in the rearview mirror. Sure, they drove him nuts, but he loved them and he knew they wouldn't be this age forever. If everything went well, it just might be a good day after all. "You kids ready? Where's your list for Santa?" Ray asked. Cindy held her list up proudly. Jimmy rolled his eyes.

"Dad, what if Santa's plane crashes? What'll happen to the presents? Who will give them out?" Jimmy asked. Cindy's jaw dropped and her eyes grew big at the thought of this happening.

"Jimmy, that's a terrible thing to say!" Sally scolded. "When we go to church tonight, I want you to think about that and pray that you don't think such awful thoughts!"

Ray Johnson smiled. He was a little more skilled at handling tough questions and he couldn't resist a chance to cruelly tease his son. "Jimmy, that's a good question. You know what will happen? If Santa's plane crashes, some of the presents will burn up. But half of them will land in the Rock River. And then they will float downstream to Rockford...then, some Negroes down on the South Side will probably take your presents out of the river and give 'em to their own kids."

"Oh Ray," Mrs. Johnson scolded. "That's not very nice. Besides, I don't think Santa will bring presents to families who judge others by where they live and the color of their skin."

Jimmy rolled his eyes, but Cindy was aghast at the thought of the demise of Santa and his precious cargo. She couldn't imagine her Barbies going to anybody besides her—certainly not to one of those "other kids" down in Rockford! Barbie wants to live at her house!

"What if Santa's parachute doesn't open?" Jimmy asked.

"Well Jimmy, you never know," Mr. Johnson said. "But if that happens, I'd say that Santa won't be working this Christmas. And those elves will have to do all the work themselves."

"Would he be back next Christmas?" Cindy asked.

"Cindy, do you remember our Uncle Dewey who was in Korea? He jumped out of planes?" Ray asked.

"No. Never met him."

"Okay. Did Uncle Dewey ever visit us at Christmas?"

"No."

"Of course not, Cindy. You know why? Because his parachute didn't open in Korea." When Ray caught a dirty look from his wife, he corrected himself. "But that won't happen to Santa today. Santa knows how to jump out of planes. He's not like your 'screwy old Uncle Dewey'."

The Johnsons pulled into the crowded North Towne Mall parking lot, with Santa's castle in sight. Sally Johnson gave her family a final inspection and hoped that their macabre conversation would be left in the car.

"Hope I can find a place to park," Ray muttered under his breath.

"Remember to lock your doors, kids. We're in Rockford now." Sally added.

◆   ◆   ◆

2,500 feet over Rockford, the skies were clear and the wind was gusting at 25 mph, perfect weather for a jump. Bill and Connie, now in full costume as Santa and his helper, gave their chutes and gear one last inspection.

Their pilot that day, Rick, called back from the cockpit and gave them their final instructions. "Well guys, you see Highway 51 down there? I am gonna circle back along there and follow the river. Then we'll be with the wind, follow me? And then we'll climb another 100 feet or so, just over the country club and the mall. Then, Connie, you jump first and then I'll wing it back east and then Bill, uh, Santa, I mean...you jump when I make a pass over the mall again."

"Gotcha, Rick," Connie said. "I've done this a few times. Just don't get us killed again like you did up at the lake!" Connie and Rick were old friends and had flown together many times, but a couple months prior, they had a close call in Lake Geneva when Rick had to make a crash landing. They walked away, but barely. Connie had broken his leg in the incident and still had to wear a steel brace. This would be his first time jumping while wearing the brace. It felt awkward and not very agile.

◆　　◆　　◆

It was an unseasonably warm day. The Johnsons made their way across the parking lot at North Towne Mall. Here, they would join the clamor of others who gathered at Santa's castle. As families got closer to the landing site, bigger kids let go of their parents' hands and pushed their way to the front, while little people sat aloft on their dad's shoulders. Suddenly, the crowd quieted as they could hear gentle roar of a small aircraft engine. With hundreds of hands carefully cupped over their eyes, children and parents of all ages looked to the sky in anticipation. Almost on cue, the crowd sang in unison:

> "Here comes Santa Claus, here comes Santa Claus! Right down Santa Claus lane!
>
> Vixen and Blitzen and all his reindeer, Pullin' on the reins!
>
> Bells are ringin', children singin', All is merry and bright!
>
> Hang your stockings and say your prayers 'Cause Santa Claus comes tonight!"

The plane looked like a small insect as it circled 3,000 feet above. Within seconds, a small speck appeared. As it separated from the plane, the shape grew more distinctive, emitting a little trail of red smoke.

"Look! I can see him!" Cindy Johnson shouted excitedly above the din of the chorus. But as spectators refocused on the sky above them, their off-key singing faded away.

Whoosh!! As he had done 1,000 times before, Connie hurled himself from the hatch of the plane. He always got a rush as the wind ripped him through the air. He felt the smoke canister discharging as he went into a freefall at 90 mph, weightlessly and effortlessly. At 2,700 feet, almost by instinct, he pulled the ripcord to activate his parachute. This time, it didn't feel right. He looked back and saw why: his parachute was caught between the smoke canister and the steel brace on his leg. He reached back and tried to free it; not an easy task, especially at the rate of speed he was falling. The wind resistance and the bundle of winter clothes Connie wore made it hard to maneuver. A tug on the rope that held the chute didn't free it from his leg and it only made matters worse. It deployed partially, but it felt like an umbrella that had been sprung inside out from a violent windstorm.

Connie breathed in the cold December air. He knew he still had a few hundred feet. After that, he'd need something better than this if he was going to land in one piece! That's what the emergency chute is for. It wasn't the first time this had happened to Connie, but it was the first time this happened when he was dressed like a goofy elf and had hundreds of kids watching. He thought of his two little girls and how they'd run over to give him a hug.

On the ground below, children cheered and pointed to the sky and the streaming red trail of smoke. From 2,400 feet, spectators couldn't tell if it was Santa or an elf. To them, it just looked like dead weight, a helpless falling object. In many respects, that's exactly what it was.

His palms soaked in sweat, Connie pulled the second ripcord to activate his emergency parachute. He felt the rigging tumble out, but it didn't fully deploy. The line got stuck on the first chute, which was still wedged between the smoke canister and the steel brace on his leg. But the faster he fell and with the wind resistance against his body, the rigging only locked in tighter. Frantically, Connie reached around to try to pull it loose. This is not easy when you're falling at 100 mph and the wind is blowing against you. He arched his back and kicked his legs, but to no avail.

In the plane circling above, Bill in his Santa suit watched in horror as his friend kept falling and falling.

"What the hell's going on down there?" the pilot asked nervously.

"He's in trouble, Rick! I'm going down!" And with that, Bill jumped. Fortunately for him, his chute would perform better when the time came.

Little Cindy Johnson still sat on her dad's shoulders, watching as the skydiving elf continued his downward spiral. The partially deployed chute looked like a U-shaped canopy, flopping violently to and fro. Ray and Sally Johnson weren't aeronautics experts, nor were most of the adults in the crowd that day, but they knew that something just didn't look right. Sally squeezed Ray's hand tighter. At that moment, the kids were distracted by the second figure they saw. The loudspeaker cackled to life. "Santa Claus is on the way!!" The announcer roared jubilantly into the microphone. Again, the children cheered. "Okay boys and girls!! The announcer bellowed, "Please turn your attention towards Santa's castle and get ready to see him when he lands. I'll bet he has lot of presents for you! Ho-Ho-Ho!!" It was a good diversion and it worked, but even the announcer knew that he'd better have his own "bag of tricks" pretty soon.

Now at 500 feet, Connie's body was soaked in sweat. As he fought, wrestled, and struggled to adjust his gear, the red smoke trail behind him took on an eerie pattern. Spectators on the ground saw Connie do a pirouette in the sky. Surely, there were those who thought that this was part of the act, but others, like Ray and Sally Johnson saw a man, somebody's husband and father, doing a death dance in midair.

Connie groaned and took his final labored breaths as the houses and roads below him grew bigger by the second.

The announcer's voice sounded nervous now, but he knew that he had to keep up his ruse that Santa was on the way. Almost on cue, the announcer stood up and waved his arms, pointing to Santa who was now gracefully descending toward them, his parachute fully deployed. "Okay, are you ready?? Let's have all the good boys and girls come over here and line up!! And let's have him hear you sing that song you sang so well before, 'Santa Claus is Coming To Town'...a one, a two, a three..." With that, the children naively broke into song. As they broke into song, three blocks away, a falling elf was about to break every bone in his body.

After the second verse of "Santa Claus is Coming to Town," the announcer looked over and spied about half of the audience looking the other way, as Connie plunged into someone's backyard. Immediately, the announcer grabbed his microphone and interrupted the children's singing. "Parents, please, please look away!! Cover your children's eyes! Please turn your attention over here to Santa's Castle!" His voice was no longer that of a happy, kid-friendly emcee. He was now a drill sergeant barking commands to his audience, and for their own good.

Rockford's Latham Street was a tranquil residential neighborhood where professional people lived in brick houses and bungalows. Dr. and Mrs. McIntosh, who lived at 3443 Latham Street, weren't home that morning, which turned out to be good timing on their part. Within seconds, their backyard became a grotesque landing pad of carnage and chaos.

Connie's body hit an oak tree first. A large branch snapped, but it did little to break his fall. His body slammed into the ground with such force that it made a crater one foot deep in the lawn. The smoke canisters still attached to his legs came off, belching out one last cloud of red smoke. Connie's body almost erupted upon impact; what were once his arms and legs, so full of life, were now little more than sacks of pulp. He never had a chance, given how far and how hard he had fallen. The Law of Gravity is merciless.

There were witnesses nearby and the one of them rushed home to call the sheriff. A couple of teenagers ran to the scene, out of curiosity. But as the teens got closer and saw Connie's lifeless body in a crater, in a pool of blood and a jumble of parachute gear, they lost their nerve and decided not to go further. If they touched him or tampered with him, something terrible might happen, and they'd never seen anything more terrible than this.

Back at North Towne Mall, the announcer told some onlookers that what they had just witnessed was nothing more than a store mannequin, and it had been dropped to test the wind. He reassured them that Santa was just fine and if they would be patient, they could see him shortly. Indeed, Bill had landed safely and was quickly ushered into the mall to change out of his Santa costume. He was very shaken and upset, as were Connie's wife and kids. Together, they were gathered and quickly escorted to the hospital.

Like clockwork, a new Santa appeared to appease the families who had been waiting all morning and who were unaware of the day's tragedy. For them, the show went on. There were some parents, however, who knew very well what happened and chose to leave. They had just lost their holiday spirit. Now they had to explain to their angry and confused children why they couldn't see Santa that day.

"Daddy, why are we going to Grandma's? Why can't we see Santa?" little Cindy asked as the Johnsons quickly left the mall. She was now sitting between her parents in the front seat of their car. This surely gave them all a sense of security, on a morning when everyone could use it.

"Uh, Santa's helper got sick. He can't help Santa today. They won't have time to see us. But he said that if we come back tomorrow instead, you'll get even more presents! How does that sound?" Ray said, looking over to his little girl for a nod of approval. He looked at Billy in the back seat, but Billy was just staring out the window, tears forming in his eyes. He heard the sirens wailing and he saw too many people leaving in panic. He wasn't buying any excuses.

"Hey, how we doing back there, Billy? Whaddaya say, let's go get some ice cream. Then we'll go over to Grandma's and work on our Christmas lists?" Ray knew that if excuses didn't work, bribery certainly would. He thought of the grisly industrial accident a few years ago at the factory, when drunken old Clyde Miller got crushed on the loading dock. Ray and his coworkers all got huge bonus checks, if they didn't talk to investigators. No, Clyde didn't live to see Christmas, but Ray and the other employees did, and financially, they all had a very nice one. Life went on.

Billy turned from the window. He dried his eyes and tousled his hair and asked, "What if Santa's helper gets sick and dies? If he was the one in charge of our presents, does that mean we won't get any presents this year?"

Mom took this question. "Of course not, Billy. If Santa's elves get old and sick, then they just have to stay home and take care of the reindeer. And yes, sometimes the elves get hurt and yes, sometimes they die, just like people do. But that doesn't mean you won't get presents. Santa just gets new elves to help him. And as long as you're good all year long and do your chores and homework, you'll still get lots of presents! We still love you and Cindy, no matter what happens to Santa and his helpers."

"Now who wants ice cream?" Dad asked. "We're almost there. Let's see who can eat the most!"

Ray and Sally looked at each other with a sly wink. Parenthood wasn't always easy, and today certainly didn't turn out the way they had expected. Accidents happen, and besides, by this time next year, probably few people would remember the skydiving elf. Regardless of what happened over the skies of Rockford that day, the Johnsons knew that in three more weeks, they would open lots of nice gifts, spend time together, and feel a sense of renewal. Isn't that what the holiday spirit is about?

Notes

The Johnson Family, with all their imperfections, are purely fictional characters.

This story is based on actual events that took place on December 5, 1965 at a promotional holiday event at Rockford's North Towne Mall. Over the years, some accounts have inaccurately reported that it was Santa Claus who perished that day. It has been referred to as the "Skydiving Santa" incident, hence the title. In fact, the victim was "Santa's helper" portrayed by Cornelius "Connie" O'Rourke, an experienced jumper and parachute instructor from Lake Geneva, Wisconsin. The other principal characters were real as well: Bill Fleming portrayed Santa Claus, and Rick Friend was their pilot.

"Chutist Dies in Holiday Program," *Morning Star* (Rockford) 5 December 1965.

"Skydiving Santa Falls To His Death," *Register Republic* (Rockford) 6 December 1965.

"FAA Seeking Cause of Skydiving Death," *Register Republic* (Rockford) 6 December 1965.

THE ROCKFORD MAFIA AND ITS PUBLIC CORRUPTION LEGACY

JEFF HAVENS

They were frequently inside or next to my Dad's lunch bucket, which was on top of the refrigerator. Usually they were stained and tattered from many days of use and exposure to harsh conditions.

At least, that's how I imagined them when I was growing up, given the fact I never saw them in use. They were just sitting there and I often looked at the covers and thumbed through their pages. At seven years in age, I could read but did not completely understand the excerpts and went on to examine the photos, if they were there. One book—or more precisely—one photo from a book, specifically left an impression on me.

The photo showed the face of a man whose eyes were bulging from their sockets. His tongue was rolling from his mouth, while a man from behind grimaced with exertion, as he worked to tighten the cord around the man's neck to squeeze the life out of his victim.

The book, of course, was the 1969 Mafia classic *The Godfather*, on which the 1972 movie masterpiece was based. The photo was a scene from the movie depicting the murder of an enforcer named Luca Brasi.

Brief history

The book and subsequent movies of the same name had a lasting impact on Americans about the inner workings of the Mob (also known as *La Cosa Nostra*) and their relationship with officials at all levels of government—local, state, and federal. While this may have been a realization for many at the time, people in the Chicago area had long been aware of the devastating effect public corruption could have on citizens' lives and democracy.

This was especially true during the era of alcohol Prohibition in the United States from 1920 to 1933 when the Mob became influential in an effort to profit from the flow of illegal drinks, such as beer and whisky. The devastation was the most obvious when organized crime syndicates shot, bombed, or killed each other or bystanders in public venues.

In response to the overt violence, organizations like the Chicago Crime Commission were formed, laws changed, and the Mob formed uneasy alliances for the betterment of their syndications, which included efforts to tap into different, if not even larger pools of money. Pools that included proceeds from international drug trafficking and local garbage collection fees, to ordinary food vending machines.

All of these items and much more are part of Rockford's long and infamous history with the Mob. To this day, many residents are unaware or ignore this history and its insidious legacy, which has now bifurcated into a more sophisticated form of public corruption while at the same time given birth to a new wave of street crime in the form of drugs, jail, and their related illegal activities that drain the community.

However, hope is not lost on the Forest City and its surrounding communities. Technological advances and relatively recent criminal prosecution efforts by former United States Attorney Patrick Fitzgerald have put a sizable dent in the Chicago-area Mob's influence and public corruption. But hope alone is not what is needed for the Rockford area to fulfill its positive potential. Action is required, and part of this action is for citizens to educate themselves about the past as a guide for a better future.

That is the purpose of this essay.

Springboard

My father used to work for a Rockford-area vending machine company, among his jobs in the 1960s through the 1980s. This was during the same time and in the same area where I grew up and first heard about the Mob from my Dad.

Not long after I started college, I read several excellent news articles one Sunday afternoon in the breakroom of Kohl's department store in Machesney Park where I worked loading and unloading trucks. It was March 4, 1984. The local daily newspaper, the *Rockford Register Star*, was bold enough to publish six news articles, eight photographs, four biographical profiles and two graphics about the Mob. One graphic was a map of the United States in which "major mob" centers were shown, including New York City, Chicago, Boston, New Orleans, Los Angeles, Las Vegas, Kansas City, Milwaukee and, of course, Rockford.

Rockford certainly has not grabbed headlines like the other cities, but as the 1984 articles aptly detailed, the local figures involved in a narcotics distribution network were targets of a criminal investigation, which would later be known as the "Pizza Connection." Understanding this multinational conspiracy, which exceeded $1 billion, is central to grasping the magnitude of challenges that face the Rockford region.

That case may be used not only as a springboard to the era prior to 1984, but also as a jumping off point in the other direction to the more recent past, when Fitzgerald spearheaded the "Family Secrets" trial in 2007.

Pizza connection

My cross-country running and track coach in high school often shuttled us to the indoor track in Sterling, Ill., for competitions in the late 1970s and early 1980s. Our trek on the way home from the facility took us on Illinois Route 2 where we usually stopped in the town of Oregon for supper at a small Italian restaurant that featured inexpensive, but excellent tasting pizza at a place called Alfano's. We never imagined that during that period, and from that restaurant, operated an expansive criminal enterprise that extended from Afghanistan, Switzerland, and Brazil to numerous pizza parlors in the United States along the East Coast and throughout the Midwest.

Fast forward 24 years to 2006 when I penned one of my last news articles for *The Rock River Times*, which was, and still is, a weekly newspaper distributed primarily in the Rockford area. I was a staff writer for the paper from October 2002 to January 2006 and contributed more news articles afterward as a special correspondent, which included the following unedited and modified version of what was published in the August 2-8, 2006 issue of the paper.

The title of the article was "Mob murder suggests link to international drug ring." It chronicles the story of a still unsolved killing of a Mob member from Rockford.

2006 article

He was found dead in the back seat of his car along Safford Road by two Winnebago County Sheriff's deputies on April 6, 1980. The victim, Rockford Mob member Joseph J. Maggio, was shot once in the side of the head at close range with 6.35mm bullet, which was made in Austria.

His killer has never been charged, and the shooting remains an open and unsolved case. However, according to Maggio's extensive FBI file, a "prime suspect" was identified by unknown sources, and the motive for his killing was "a result of his objection to LCN [*La Cosa Nostra*] entry into the narcotics business in Rockford." And according to an October 1984 FBI document, an unknown informant "was instructed by his 'associates' in either Las Vegas or Los Angeles that Maggio had to be killed. [Redacted] 'associates' are members of the LCN."

Maggio's murder and FBI file provides another piece to the puzzle that may one day directly link Rockford to the Mafia-run heroin and cocaine smuggling conspiracy of the 1970s and 1980s, which was known as the "Pizza Connection."

Of the nearly 1,500 pages *The Rock River Times* requested from Maggio's FBI file, only 90 pages were released by the U.S. Justice Department. Most of the 90 pages released were heavily redacted or censored for content.

However, the information that was released shows the Mob's determination to not only scam ordinary citizens out of money through businesses that appear completely legitimate, but also gain access to FBI files.

Origins

Less than two months before Maggio was killed, he and other Mafia members met "several times" in February 1980 with Rockford Mob boss Joseph Zammuto in Ft. Lauderdale, Fla. — where Zammuto vacationed during the winter each year.

Exactly what was discussed at the meeting is not known. However, Maggio's heavily redacted file indicates an unknown individual or group "began dealing narcotics in Rockford in August 1980, with Zammuto's sanction."

As to who began dealing drugs with Zammuto's approval is not known because of the redactions. However, what is known is John S. Leombruni was convicted in 1983 for trafficking cocaine in Rockford and the surrounding area.

According to a March 4, 1984 article in the *Rockford Register Star*, "There were indications in 1982 that a six-month investigation by the FBI of cocaine traffic in Rockford had turned up mob connections. Twelve persons were indicted, including John S. Leombruni, who was described as the city's biggest cocaine dealer. ... Leombruni had lived in Las Vegas the year before his arrest."

And according to the *Register Star* article, an FBI affidavit indicated, Leombruni "was run out of town by 'the Mafia chief in Las Vegas.' Court approved wiretaps showed mob involvement in the Rockford cocaine case FBI agents said, but were not allowed as evidence in Leombruni's trial." He was tried in federal court in Rockford.

These sequence of incidents from published sources, suggests a strong link between the Rockford Mob and other participants in the Pizza Connection whose second in command for Midwest operations was Oregon, Ill., pizza maker Pietro Alfano.

According to a source for *The Rock River Times*, Alfano "retired" and returned to Sicily shortly after his release from federal prison in 1992. As of 2004, Alfano's son operated the restaurant, which was still in business in Oregon.

Ralph Blumenthal, reporter for The New York Times and author of the 1988 book *Last Days of the Sicilians*, wrote that Alfano immigrated to the United States between 1963 and 1967 from Cinisi, Sicily, a town about 8 miles west of Palermo near the Mediterranean Sea.

Cinisi was also the hometown of former Sicilian Mob boss Gaetano Badalamenti, who was born in 1923, and died in 2004. Badalamenti became head of the Sicilian Mafia in 1969, but fled for his life to Brazil in November 1978 in the wake of the "Mafia wars" in Sicily.

Alfano and other Mob members born in Sicily, but working in United States, were referred to as "Zips" by their American-born counterparts. According to Selwyn Raab, former New York Times reporter and author of the 2005 book *Five Families: The Rise, Decline and Resurgence of America's Most Powerful Mafia Empires*, the term "Zip" may be Sicilian slang for "hicks" or "primitives."

Drugs and intelligence files

On April 8, 1984, Alfano and Badalamenti were apprehended by police in Madrid, Spain. Authorities charged that they, along with 29 others overseas and in the United States, participated in a multinational, $1.65 billion heroin/cocaine smuggling and money laundering conspiracy.

The conspiracy stretched from poppy fields in Afghanistan to banks in Switzerland, ships in Bulgaria and Turkey, pay phones in Brazil, and pizza restaurants in New York, Oregon, Ill., and Milton, Wis. The conspiracy would become known as the "Pizza Connection," the successor to the 1950s and 1960s "French Connection."

In 2006, when the article was published, Dominic Iasparro was Winnebago County Sheriff's Department deputy chief, former interim chief of the Rockford Police Department and head of the Rockford area Metro Narcotics task force. He had been with the agency about 32 years.

Iasparro recalled area drug trafficking during the time of the Pizza Connection and said: "As I understand it, the drugs weren't coming out here—they were staying in New York".". Iasparro said this during an April 12, 2004 interview.

Frankly, I was shocked when Iasparro made the statement and still find it comical for its astonishing and exceedingly significant level of naiveté, given Iasparro's vast law enforcement experience and apparently keen knowledge of narcotics distribution. And he offered more astounding information that was in the article:

In addition to being former head of the local narcotics unit, Iasparro was also responsible for destroying police intelligence files concerning Rockford Mob members in the mid-1980s that Iasparro claimed was part of a nationwide effort to purge such information. Maggio's dossier was among the files requested by *The Rock River Times* in 2005, but apparently destroyed during the purge.

Immigration and sponsorship

Under what circumstances Alfano arrived in the United States is not clear. However, what is clear is Alfano and his cohorts in the Midwest and on the East Coast were employed in the pizza business. Also apparent is former Rockford Mob boss Frank J. Buscemi was reported by the *Register Star* to have facilitated the immigration of "several cousins to Rockford from Sicily and set them up in business."

What is not certain is whether Buscemi, a Chicago native, sponsored Alfano's move to Illinois. Buscemi was owner of Stateline Vending Co., Inc., and Rondinella Foods Co., before his death in Rockford on Dec. 7, 1987. Rondinella was a wholesale cheese, food, and pizza ingredient distributor.

Stateline Vending began operating from the basement of the Aragona Club on Kent Street before moving to 1128 S. Winnebago St., which was owned by former Mafia Advisor Joseph Zito and Mob member Jasper Calo. The vending business eventually settled at 326 W. Jefferson St., in Rockford, before it was dissolved in 1988, after Buscemi's death.

Winnebago County court documents from 1988 indicate alleged Rockford Mob hit man Frank G. Saladino worked for Rondinella in the 1980s when Buscemi owned the business. Saladino was reportedly found dead April 25, 2005 in Hampshire, Ill., by federal agents that went to arrest him on charges of murder and other illegal Mob-related activities.

According to Buscemi's FBI file, Buscemi was also the target of a federal investigators from 1981 to 1986 in connection with Maggio's murder and "extortionate business practices."

"These allegations involved Buscemi's cheese distribution business, RONDINELLA FOODS, and his vending machine operation, STATE-LINE VENDING." Buscemi's file also indicates that the investigation produced "numerous leads of extreme value, including contacts between Frank J. Buscemi and the subject of an ongoing Boston drug task force investigation."

Despite the years of investigations, Buscemi was never charged with any crime before his death in 1987. Also unknown is whether Zammuto's only sister, whose married name is Alfano, was related to Pietro Alfano through marriage.

Business meeting

The Mob's historic ties to the vending machine business is significant in establishing an indirect link between the Rockford Mob and the Pizza connection because of a meeting that took place in July 1978 in Milwaukee between Mob members from New York, Milwaukee and Rockford.

In July 1978, federal court documents show Rockford Mafia Advisor Joseph Zito, Mob Underboss Charles Vince, and Phillip J. Emordeno, along with other members of the Milwaukee, and New York Mafia, were alleged to have tried to extort money from a competing upstart vending machine company owner. The owner of the company the Mob members tried to shakedown, was actually an undercover federal agent named Gail T. Cobb who was masquerading as Tony Conte, owner of Best Vending Co.

According to page 229 of Raab's book, legendary FBI agent Donnie Brasco, whose real name was Joseph P Pistone, was "used" by Bonanno Mob soldier Benjamin "Lefty Guns" Ruggiero "on cooperative ventures with other families in New York, Florida and Milwaukee."

Blumnenthal wrote on page 42 of his book that in 1978 Pistone traveled to Milwaukee to vouch for Cobb, and "Pistone helped Cobb cement an alliance between the Bonanno and [Milwaukee Mob boss Frank P.] Balistrieri clans."

Actor Johnny Depp portrayed Pistone in the 1997 movie *Donnie Brasco*, during the time in the late 1970s when Pistone infiltrated organized crime ("Lefty Guns" Ruggiero was played by Al Pacino).

The *Register Star* described the 1978 meeting in their March 1984 article as being partly arranged by Rockford Mob members. The article concluded the meeting "confirmed long-held intelligence information that … [the Rockford Mob] possessed the influence to deal directly with the Milwaukee and New York organized crime families." The meeting was set to quash a possible violent conflict between Cobb and Mafia members.

Ruggerio's Mob captain, Michael Sa Bella contacted Tony Riela—a New Jersey Mob member with ties to the Rockford Mafia. Riela called Rockford to schedule the meeting, and Ruggiero called Zito several times. Vince also called Balistrieri's son J. Peter Balisrieri shortly before the meeting.

According to the *Register Star* article, "on July 29, 1978 Cobb met the three Rockford men and Ruggiero at the Centre Stage Restaurant in Milwaukee. …. Ruggiero told Cobb that the vending machine business in Milwaukee was controlled by the Mob," and if Cobb wanted to enter the business he would have to share his profits with the Mafia or be killed. Since the New York and Milwaukee crime families worked together, "Cobb also was told he would have to pay a portion of his profits to the Bonanno family," which was headed at that time by Carmine "Lilo" Galante.

Death on the patio

Blumenthal wrote that the shotgun assignation of Galante in the mid-afternoon on July 12, 1979 while he was dining on the patio of a restaurant in Brooklyn, N.Y., marked a tipping point in the power struggle to control drug trafficking in America. Pizza Connection prosecutors believed Galante's murder "cleared the way for Sicilian Mafia rivals in America to set up the Pizza Connection."

Raab said on page 207 that Galante attempted to injure the other four New York Mob family's interests in the drug trade, especially the Gambino crime family. "Perhaps even more grievous, after Carlo Gambino's death [Galante] had openly predicted that he would be crowned boss of bosses."

Although Frank Balistrieri and others would be sent to prison as a result of Cobb and Pistone's efforts, no Rockford Mob members were indicted in the Milwaukee case. The same may also be said about the Pizza Connection conspiracy.

Shooting on the sidewalk

Unlike Galante, Alfano survived a Mob attempt on his life.

After emerging from a Balducci's delicatessen in Greenwhich Village, N.Y. the evening of Feb. 11, 1987, Alfano was shot three times in the back by two men who emerged from a red car. The shooting occurred during the October 1985 to March 1987 Pizza Connection trial.

Blumenthal wrote the failed assassination attempt was allegedly arranged by Gambino family associates, which left Alfano paralyzed below the waist and confined to a wheel chair.

Blumenthal alleged Salvatore Spatola, a convicted heroin and cocaine smuggler, said the attempted killing of Alfano had been arranged by Pasquale Conte, Sr.— a captain in the Gambino family.

The exact motive for Alfano's shooting appears to be a mystery. However, Blumenthal wrote that convicted New Jersey bank robber Frank Bavosa told the FBI and New York police he and two other men were paid $40,000 to kill Alfano "allegedly because of his continuing drug-trafficking activities."

Autonomous but united

Even though the Rockford Mob has historically been considered part of the Chicago Mafia, which is known as "The Outfit," Tommaso Buscetta, Sicilian Mafia turncoat and lead witness in the Pizza Connection trial testified that Italian-based Mobsters based throughout the world acted as one in achieving their objectives.

Supporting that claim is a statement from Thomas V. Fuentes, special agent in the organized crime section for the FBI. During a 2003 broadcast on the History Channel, Fuentes said a Nov. 14, 1957 meeting of Mafia bosses from throughout the United States in Apalachin, N.Y., was in part to decide whether American Mob members would act cohesively to cash in on the drug trade.

Specifically, Fuentes said: "We believe that the main purpose was for the bosses of the American families to decide whether or not they would engage jointly in heroin trafficking with their cousins in Sicily."

Rockford Mob Consuleri Joseph Zito's brother, Frank Zito, boss of the Springfield, Ill., Mob was one of those who attended the Apalachin conference, according to Joseph Zito's FBI file.

Also in attendance at the Apalachin meeting with Zito were at least 58 other Mob members, which included Carlo Gambino; Vito Genovese, boss of the New York Genovese crime family; Gambino's brother-in-law Paul Castellano; and Joe Bonanno. Castellano would be Gambino's successor after Gambino's death in 1976. Castellano was murdered in 1986, and was succeeded by John Gotti, who died in a Missouri prison medical center June 10, 2002.

Scam in Alabama

In addition to a probable motive for Maggio's killing, Maggio's FBI file shows Mob's determination to not only steal money from citizens, but gain access to FBI files.

Maggio was convicted on Dec. 6, 1972 on seven counts of mail fraud and one count of conspiracy. The conviction was obtained after an unidentified male informant said the conspiracy involved a "boat registration scheme", wherein the name United States Merchant Marine was used to collect funds for a national boat registration service.

"He said they planned to circulate a letter to all boat owners for a $10 contribution, which would then be used as a registration fee for a registry to be maintained by the company [United States Merchant Marine Service, Inc.]. ...

"[Redact] had asked him if he had any idea how the United States Merchant Marine Service could patch into the Federal Bureau of Investigation (FBI) National Crime Information Center (NCIC)."

Maggio was born Aug. 30, 1936 in Rockford, where he lived his entire life, until his death at age 43. Maggio married in 1959, and had three sons and one daughter. He became a made Mob member in approximately February 1965.

The trash man and his cohorts

This is everything I know about the Pizza Connection that can be printed. I strongly encourage interested readers to visit the library and read the March 4, 1984 news articles in the *Rockford Register Star*. It was printed at a time when the daily paper actually practiced investigative journalism, before devolving into the shallow stenographers and tweeters of today.

I also highly recommend you visit *The Rock River Times* website to read my own articles on the Mob and public corruption. And I would be remiss if I did not give a tip of the hat to Brandon Reid and Frank Schier of *The Rock River Times* for editing and publishing my articles to offer this public service of disseminating such needed information.

If you have read this far into the essay, three figures now become key in better understanding more recent developments on the evolution of the Mob and public corruption in Rockford, from sanctioned executions to questionable public contracts. Those figures are accused hitman Frank Saladino, alleged member Salvatore "Sam" Galluzzo, and reputed Counsuleri Jospeh Zito.

According one of the 1984 articles titled: "In pursuit of 'Diamond Joe'; FBI trailed Joseph Zito across the country for a decade," Zito was born in Italy, his brothers settled in Rockford and Springfield, Ill., and he "came to Rockford from Springfield during Prohibition along with his brother-in-law Jasper Calo who became underboss of the Rockford mob." Zito was investigated for years for his involvement in gambling, liquor, and municipal garbage services.

An article I wrote that accompanied one of several garbage stories I penned about ten years ago for *The Rock River Times* summarized some of these activities to give readers perspective about the past. From the Dec. 14-20, 2005 issue, the article reads as follows with minor modifications:

2005 article

Zito's FBI file includes allegations of bribery and intimidation during a time when a new garbage contract was being negotiated in the late 1960s and early 1970s. During that time, the city closed the municipally-owned People's Avenue landfill and began dumping its trash at the privately-owned Pagel Pit, which opened in July 1972.

The dump, which was formerly known as Pagel Pit, received approval from the Winnebago County Board Dec. 8, 2005 to expand Winnebago Landfill. The 18.7 million cubic-yard expansion is expected to serve 11 northern Illinois counties between 2010 and 2031.

In 2004, the county also approved spending millions of taxpayer funds on two roads that lead to the landfill. The money will pay for 8 miles of road upgrades on Baxter Road and 5 miles on South Perryville Road.

According to the FBI file, Zito was allegedly part owner of the City of Rockford's former waste hauler Rockford Disposal Service Co. A March 31, 1970, FBI bulletin from Zito's FBI file reads that a male source said "[redact] for the Rockford Disposal Company and is also [redact] the Greater Rockford Airport Authority.

"He said the site, which was under consideration as a new landfill site to be used for dumping garbage was under control of the airport authority and although unsuitable, in [redact] opinion, as a landfill site was being pushed in the City Council when the Illinois State Health Department advised that it would not be approved by that department as a landfill site.

"[Redact] advised that the City furnished the landfill site for the contractor who has the garbage disposal contact for Rockford, Illinois.

"[Redact] said that in conversation with [redact] they stated no matter which site was selected for the landfill and no matter who the current contractor might be they would have to make their peace with Rockford Disposal Company.'

"He said he asked what was meant by that statement but received no answer. ... when he was showing opposition to the airport landfill site, he was approached by [redact] Rockford Disposal Company, in approximately October 1969, was asked, "'What does it take to get you to leave us alone?'" wrote the unidentified FBI agent.

Less than two months after issuing that memorandum, the FBI issued another bulletin on May 13, 1970. The document concerned alleged "bribery negotiations relative to [the] Cherry Valley Landfill site."

The bulletin reads: "[A source] states he was told it would cost $100,000 to obtain Rockford City Disposal contract.

"It has been previously reported that sources believe Rockford Disposal Service, Inc., utilizes Joe Zito in quieting labor disputes when Rockford Disposal first obtained the Rockford City contract [in 1956]. ...

"Rockford is presently attempting to locate a landfill site which would then be used by Rockford Disposal in performance of its trash removal contract. ... The site most likely to be chosen is located in Cherry Valley Township, adjacent to Rockford."

During a Dec. 1, 2005 interview, Dave Johnson, Winnebago County Clerk and former long-time Rockford alderman, said he thought the site referred to in Zito's FBI file was the City of Rockford's 155-acre composting facility at the northeast corner of South Mulford and Baxter roads.

Johnson raised questions about the city's garbage contract in 1974, which led to an investigation conducted by the Rockford Police Department. According to a 1975 Rockford Police Department report, Browning Ferris Industries, the city's garbage hauler at that time, was also known as Rockford Disposal Service Co. State records indicate Rockford Disposal changed its name to Laidlaw Waste Systems (Illinois) Inc., on March 25, 1982.

When Zito died in 1981, an FBI surveillance photo shows Zito's funeral was attended by Chicago Mafia boss Joseph Aiuppa, Joseph Zammuto, head of the Rockford Mob, and Frank J. Buscemi, who took control from Zammuto after his retirement, according to a March 4, 1984, *Rockford Register Star* article.

Rockford and its smelly garbage contracts

Using this information as a guide, a reporter and astute reader would rightfully cast a skeptical eye on any trash contracts, and I certainly did, especially after I rediscovered the 1984 articles sometime in 2004.

But before that in October 2002, one of my first articles for *The Rock River Times* was about a dubious change to the City of Rockford's garbage service contract. During my research for the article, I began plotting numbers from past ordinances to compare and understand why city officials extended the contract from five years to 10 years. The ordinances in question had few details other than rates in dollars for each year. It was the rates and time periods that raised my suspicion and I discovered the motive in the graphics.

From my advanced algebra courses, I knew what the differing financial interest formulas looked like when plotted on a graph. The old ordinance from the early 1990s covered five years. The data showed the method used to compute the old contract appeared to be a piecewise function. In other words, there did not appear to be a logical formula followed to determine rates in the 1990 ordinance.

However, whoever crafted the new Rockford garbage contract for the periods between 1995 through 2004 seemed to know exactly what they were doing when the time frame was extended from five years to ten because of something bankers call compound interest. In a compound interest contract, the bulk of the money is earned at the end of the contract, not the beginning or middle.

This was explained in the October 2002 article: "City garbage disposal contract smells." It began: "At best, Rockford may be overpaying hundreds of thousands of dollars for the disposal of refuse, more likely millions, for the years 2002-2004, if the current ordinance/contract is not renegotiated.

"The question revolves around the difference between using a simple interest formula or a compound interest formula, whether 6 percent interest is fair, and if Winnebago Reclamation, Inc., is willing to renegotiate the present ordinance/contract, which runs from 1995-2004.

"In addition, the city's failure to address contingencies in the refuse disposal ordinance/contract, appears to put the City of Rockford at a disadvantage."

Like many public contracts, the proverbial devil was in the details and it was obvious this was the case with the language used in the 2000 city budget to sell the extended contract, and the contract contingencies, such as types of waste allowed to be dumped, lack of audits of the dump and unverifiable favored rates for dumping.

In other words, no one supposedly dumps, and is charged, at a rate less than what the city receives—the city theoretically gets the lowest rate. The problem was no one could actually verify the important terms of the contract, which leads us to the City of Loves Park's contract that smelled as equally bad.

The Loves Park odor

More garbage articles appeared in 2005 that prompted City of Loves Park attorney Paul S. Nicolosi to tersely respond to me in e-mails. The e-mails were the alternative, since Nicolosi insisted on interview restrictions.

From the Dec. 14-20, 2005 issue, I wrote: "Significant problems with Rockford and Loves Park's garbage contracts still exist 10 months after *The Rock River Times* research suggested the pacts may be costing taxpayers and residents big money. Exactly how much money is not possible to calculate under the existing system.

"Both cities have no way to compare and verify that the municipality is receiving the lowest possible rate for collection and/or disposal of garbage, as stipulated in the contracts.

"The primary issue focuses on different and incompatible units that are used to determine payments for garbage collection and disposal services. Specifically, Rockford pays the contractor in dollars per ton of refuse, and Loves Park residents pay the contractor in dollars per residential unit. But both cities' contracts are with subsidiary companies of William Charles, Inc. ...

"During an interview Feb. 9, 2005, Loves Park Mayor Darryl F. Lindberg admitted it wasn't possible for residential owners to determine if they are receiving the lowest rate. He also said he was very happy with the level of service Rock River Disposal has provided since the contract went into effect Jan. 1, 2003.

"Lindberg said during the February interview that Loves Park's contract was negotiated by City Attorney Paul S. Nicolosi.

"Through a series of e-mails, Nicolosi refused requests for an unrestricted interview. Nicolosi insisted on receiving a list of the questions and topics before any interview.

"*The Rock River Times* declined Nicolosi's proposal, but did submit unanswered questions regarding the February 2005 article.

"In Nicolosi's final e-mail Nov. 21, [2005,] he responded to a question about whether he personally read Loves Park's garbage contract before entering into the agreement by writing:

"'Jeff, are you serious? I did answer the question. We look at all major contracts for our municipal clients when asked to do so. This is a major contract, and it is my recollection that we where [sic, were] asked to and did in fact look at it. Again, I was attempting to be more inclusive to your question.

"'I have spoken to my client [the City of Loves Park] and have been informed that they have no issue with the contract, that the current contractor was the low bidder, the service is excellent, it is on a per household, not tonnage basis.

"'My client has further asked that I spend no further time unless specific and supportable facts are set out to call the fairness of the award process and contract into question. As such I am ethically required to follow no further on this matter. I hope that the above answers your question,' Nicolosi wrote.

"Nicolosi cut off questions before he was asked whether he was instructed by Lindberg to spend no further time answering questions concerning the contract."

Interesting links

Given Nicolosi's dealings with Loves Park's garbage contract, another article appeared in that same December 2005 issue that linked directly back to alleged Mob figure Salvatore Galluzzo, who was business partners accused hitman Frank Saladino.

The story reads: Nicolosi, "City of Loves Park attorney and owner of the law firm Nicolosi and Associates, P.C. refused an unrestricted interview concerning Loves Park's garbage contract and his business associates. Nicolosi was business partners with alleged Mob soldier Salvatore 'Sam' Galluzzo in the development firm Buckley Partners LLC.

"Galluzzo was identified as an alleged Mob member in a March 4, 1984, article published by the *Rockford Register Star*.

"During former Illinois Gov. George Ryan's term, owners of Buckley Partners—Nicolosi, Galluzzo and Galluzzo's brother Natale Gallluzzo—were recipients of at least two state contracts. The contracts were detailed in the June 22-28, 2005, issue of *The Rock River Times*.

"One of those contracts was between the Illinois Attorney General's office and Buckley Partners, which leased office space for the attorney general's regional headquarters at 7230 Argus Drive in Rockford." ...

Yes, you read that last few paragraphs correctly. The Attorney General for the State of Illinois was renting office space from a company that included an alleged Mob soldier.

The article continued: "In addition to being part owner of Buckley Partners and attorney for the City of Loves Park, Nicolosi is the attorney for the villages of Rockton and Caledonia. David Kurlinkus, an attorney at Nicolosi and Associates, is also the attorney for the Village of Roscoe. ...

"Galluzzo was business partners with alleged Mob hit-man Frank G. Saladino in Worldwide General Contracting Inc. However, the City of Rockford never issued any building permits to Worldwide General Contracting since it was founded in 1988.

"According to the Kane County coroner, Saladino was found dead of natural causes in a rural Kane County hotel room April 25, [2005], the same day he was indicted on federal charges of murder and other undisclosed criminal allegations."

But the Saladino allegations, along with interesting photos, were later disclosed in 2007 during the landmark trial known as "Family Secrets" in Chicago where Dominic Iasparro contributed his testimony.

Family secrets

Almost two years after I left employment with the paper, I continued to write for *The Rock River Times* as an unpaid public service and special correspondent. Below is an edited version of the article that appeared in the Oct. 3-10, 2007 issue:

Although the federal jury in Chicago handed down racketeering convictions in the historic Chicago Mafia trial and is deliberating murder charges, there are many questions locals may never have answered anytime soon. This revelation comes in spite of a local law enforcement official's participation in the monumental investigation and resulting trial of the Chicago Mob.

Dominic Iasparro, deputy chief of the Winnebago County Sheriff's Department, said he testified for about 15 minutes Aug. 1, 2007, during which he identified three Rockford men in photographs the prosecution introduced earlier as exhibits.

"I participated in the [Operation Family Secrets] investigation, and was subpoenaed to identify a series of photographs," Iasparro said.

When asked about his role in the investigation, Iasparro declined to provide any details. The multi-year investigation led to the 2005 indictment of 14 individuals connected to the Mob on charges that included murder, conspiracy, racketeering, illegal gambling and loan sharking, from the 1960s to the time of the indictment.

"According to Iasparro, the individuals he identified were Saladino, Salvatore Galluzzo and Joseph W. Saladino." ...

Iasparro is the same man who said he was responsible for destroying Rockford Police Department Mob files and thought that drugs involved with the "Pizza Connection" conspiracy were staying in New York.

"Although Frank Saladino was charged with murder and other undisclosed crimes, he was never tried because he was found dead in a hotel room the day he was indicted, April 25, 2005. And even though their names and photos were mentioned during the trial, Joseph Saladino and Galluzzo were not charged in connection with the 'Family Secrets' operation.

"Several photos featuring both Saladinos and Galluzzo were submitted during the federal government's case against the Mob. One FBI surveillance photo taken April 20, 1989, shows Salvatore Galluzzo leading Frank Saladino in a parking lot." ...

Saladino apparently had a falling out with his associates because he filed at least one known lawsuit against them in federal court.

In connection with Worldwide General Contracting, Phil Nicolosi was named in 2000 as a defendant in a lawsuit in which Frank Saladino alleged extortion, conspiracy, and fraud against him and 13 others, including Paul Nicolosi and Salvatore Galluzzo.

The 2007 article reads: "Phil Nicolosi speculated he was named in the lawsuit because Frank Saladino did not have proper representation advising him, 'he may have felt that he should just name as many names as he could.'

"Paul Nicolosi has responded to repeated questions in the last few years about his association with Galluzzo by not commenting," the article closed.

At the time this essay was being written, I was given notice that on Jan. 6, 2014, Philip J. Nicolosi was scheduled to be the next associate judge for the Rockford-area Judicial Circuit. He was also Winnebago County State's Attorney from 2007 to 2008.

Light sentence

Joseph Saladino served 27 months in a Minnesota prison for a conviction on federal weapons charges, including possession of a machine gun.

He could have received up to 10 years in prison and a $250,000 fine on the charges. Instead, he pled guilty in federal court in 2003 to possession of the machine gun and possession of a firearm by a felon.

As part of the plea agreement, Saladino served a little more than two years in prison in spite of his violent past, which included battery of a police officer in 1983, obstructing a police officer about one month later and a 1964 rape conviction along with co-perpetrator Frank Saladino.

The 2003 agreement for Joe Saladino was negotiated by Rockford-based Assistant U.S. Attorney Michael F. Iasparro, son of Dominic Iasparro.

In a Rockford-area case that was likely related to the "Family Secrets" operation, Joseph Saladino and Frank Saladino were named in February 2006, along with eight others in an alleged illegal sports betting ring that existed from the early 1980s until 2002. Most individuals that were indicted in that case pled guilty to the federal charges.

Land deals and distribution

Clout and links also appear to factor into other businesses, besides ruse vending machine companies in Milwaukee and general contracting companies in Rockford that were never issued a building permit. The next Rockford business was, and still is, operating that has links that I will start with by going back to 1968.

In December 1968, a federal grand jury in Freeport called at least eight people in for questioning in connection with illegal gambling and other Mob-related activity in Rockford and northern Illinois.

Among those subpoenaed before the Freeport grand jury were: Rockford Mob boss Joseph Zammuto, adviser Joseph Zito, underboss Charles Vince, Zammuto's alleged successor, Frank J. Buscemi, Philip Priola Sr., and Mob Soldier Joseph J. Maggio.

Vince was identified in the March 1984, *Rockford Register Star* article as residing in an apartment at 1904 Auburn St., in Rockford. Land records for the address show the property was owned by the grandparents of Peter and Mathew Provenzano from 1964 to 1987.

As stated earlier in this essay, in July 1978, federal court documents show Vince, along with other members of the Rockford and Milwaukee Mafia, were alleged to have tried to extort money from a competing upstart vending machine company owner. The owner of the company the Mob members tried to shakedown was actually an undercover federal agent named Gail Cobb who was masquerading as Tony Conte.

As to Vince's residence and the Provenzano family's ownership of the property, Peter Provenzano was given the opportunity in October 2005 to comment about this coincidence, his business and home rule questions, but declined after he was given an advance copy of topics for the interview (see article, "Home rule proponent Provenzano dodges TRRT interview" from the Oct. 19-25, 2005, issue of *The Rock River Times*).

Provenzano was a board commissioner at Rockford/Chicago International Airport, proponent for Rockford's return to home rule, and part owner of military contractor SupplyCore, Inc. Since its incorporation in 1987 as Pro Technical Products, Inc., the companies have been awarded more than $1 billion in U.S. Defense Department contracts—most of which has been awarded since the late 1990s.

Pro Technical Products, which was formed by Provenzano's father, changed its name to SupplyCore in 2001, according to state records. Provenzano's brother, Mathew Provenzano, was secretary of SupplyCore and was one of the board of directors for the taxpayer-supported MetroCentre in Rockford.

Both Provenzano brothers were nominated for their positions by Rockford Mayor Larry Morrissey. SupplyCore heavily financed Morrissey's first mayoral campaign.

In July 2005, I reported reputed Mob associate and millionaire Nick S. Boscarino of South Barrington, Ill., purchased a local pizza restaurant and land in Loves Park. At the time, Boscarino was serving time in federal prison on fraud charges for bilking the Village of Rosemont of money related to undisclosed insurance fees.

Boscarino purchased the former Cannova's restaurant and adjacent property at 200-204 E. Riverside Blvd., on March 15, 2005 for $150,000. He also bought 2.79 acres of vacant commercial and residential land in April 2004 near the intersection of Clinton and Windsor roads for $150,000 from AMCORE blind trust 79-7247.

In October 2004, Boscarino acquired 6.32 acres of undeveloped farmland in unincorporated Winnebago County about 1,400 feet south of the intersection of Perryville and Harlem roads. County records indicate Boscarino paid $180,000 for the land to another blind trust numbered 2700282 from the Chicago Title Land Trust Company.

Also in 2005, *The Rock River Times* revealed Edolo J. "Zeke" Giorgi, former Rockford alderman and state representative, once worked for a Mob-owned distributing company. The now defunct Northern Illinois Music, Inc./Midwest Distributing Company in Rockford was partially owned by Chicago Mafia members William Daddano Jr., and Anthony A. Cardamone.

Giorgi died in October 1993 and part of Interstate 39 was named after him in 2003 for his legislative efforts to construct the road.

Perspective

Had I stayed at the paper, I would have researched more about Giorgi, investigated the interactions of political contributions and public contracts, and followed up on stories already published.

But that fall, I decided to accept a job in northern Wisconsin, change careers and return to work in the environmental health field. However, as I stated earlier, I did update stories until 2007 when I decided the baton had to be passed.

Critics of my articles argued I unfairly targeted people primarily because of their links concerning business associates and money, which included numerous and varied political campaign contributions. I would counter that such contributions, businesses, and associations are the current engine of public corruption.

The purpose of the news editing process and journalism is to provide readers with the most accurate perspective possible through known facts. Yes, mistakes can be made, but time, diligence, and further information should eventually provide the prism and focus needed to brightly illuminate nefarious public activities in which they can, and should be sanitized, under the intense light of public disclosure. Frank Schier and Brandon Reid, the editor and assistant editor, respectively, at *The Rock River Times* aptly provided this safeguard for each and every article that was published.

I read somewhere that politics is the peaceful alternative to violent, physical conflict and deadly war, which seems to be a logical assessment. But my observations suggest politics also can give birth to a differing type of war and conflict in the form of monetary destruction and fiscal assassination. I believe this is the new tool for the public corruption network in Rockford: financial retribution and unwarranted, negative and disproportionate consequences that accompany a coordinated attack on the victim that challenges the status quo.

In other words, the old ways of the Mob are pretty much dead.

It has changed and merged into a network of public corruption that feeds at the trough of large pools of public money; from defense contractors who are needlessly paid huge sums of money for being nothing more than middle-men to vastly overpriced construction of public facilities, and ruse contracts that lead people to believe they are getting a fair deal.

When—or in the case of Rockford, if—people discover they are being taken for a ride, they are understandably angry about the deception and loss of money, which can breed cynicism, contempt, and suspicion that hamstrings the democratic process. Many in Rockford rightfully feel this about the network that is, and has been, in control for too many years.

But times have changed and the pendulum of power can shift back to the people through advances in technology. Thankfully, the overt violence that dominated the Prohibition era has died, but apparently has been replaced with straight-up, white-collar crime and the more sinister legalized crime and rackets, through strange ordinances and bizarre statutes created by slimy attorneys, unscrupulous politicians and greasy bankers bent on personal gain, rather than stewardship for the public good.

For example, in the old days, people down on their financial luck used to go to the Mob for loans, if they couldn't get money from a bank or earn enough from work. In return for the money, the Mob charged ridiculous amounts of interest on the loan, which left people in debt for a long, long time for what originally might have been a small amount of cash.

Today, the bankers at the cash store on nearly every corner in Rockford are the ones charging the exorbitant interest rates. The cash store people will argue they are regulated, fill a void in the financial sector, and provide a valuable service to their clients. But that's a small pool of private money, in relative terms.

If one examines any big pool of public money, there is little doubt in my mind there will be a long and tangled trail of seedy campaign contributions, slippery politicians, and questionable business associations leading to deceptive contracts, sleazy ordinances and sordid statutes that pilfer the accounts of Mr. and Ms. John Q. and Jane Q. Public.

They appear to take their lead from the guys and gals on Wall Street who plunged the world's economy down the toilet and into the sewers of the Great Recession. This is the primordial cesspool from which the Rockford area must emerge to evolve its positive potential.

We reside in the United States; land of hope and opportunity. We need not compare ourselves to the lowest common denominator of worldwide public corruption and collectively say: "We may have problems, but not anything like that."

No, in this country, the power is still in the hands of the people, but that grip has been slipping, as mighty, multinational corporations are now considered people with identical free-speech rights that are essentially on a much higher plain than individual humans who eventually die and have a tiny amount of wealth, in comparative terms.

Rockford and other communities must act to preserve, protect, and retrieve the public sector for the common good through peaceful means at the ballot box, community activism, and other appropriate efforts. This is exactly what was done during Prohibition when community members formed the Chicago Crime Commission when police failed to curb the violence and intimidation because key police officials, judges and politicians were in the clutches of the Mob.

I began this essay with a goal of education through history. I believe the goal was achieved and my hope is this education leads to action for a better future in the Rockford area. Perhaps one day there will be a well-worn book on a table in Rockford that details such success that was read by a father during his lunch break at work, and his young son will see a photo in the book of a smiling group of community leaders who had the best interest of the citizens in mind when they acted.

ROCKFORD OPERETTA PARTY

AN UNDISCOVERED GEM

SCOTT FARRELL

Among many performing acts in Rockford, opera tends to be on the fringe of the community. Although an opera house existed downtown in the 1900s, opera became more obscure until the art form was dropped from many venues altogether. It only occasionally appeared in Mendelssohn Club programming or the Starlight Theatre productions of the 1980s. Otherwise, fans had to travel to another city for the opera experience. In the early part of the 21st Century, however, for a brief period opera seemed to have a chance at rebirth in the community. Although many classical musicians in the area are aware of the Coronado productions of *Die Fledermaus* in 2003 and *La Boheme* in 2006, there was another side of opera that filled the rest of the decade. That was the performing group I started.

I was born in 1980 at Rockford Memorial Hospital, and began my musical journey at East High School in the mid-1990s. Later, I studied piano with Inger Langsholt and Dean Durst, and entered the world of theatre through George Harnish. Upon the latter's production of *The Mikado* (1998), I took an immense interest in light opera, and very soon started my own performing group. My first production was an original play with music titled *The Princess' Lament*, performed as part of Rock Valley College's Drama Workshop in 1999. It was followed the next summer with another premiere in *The Sapphire Necklace*, also by myself. The group became known as the Royal English Opera Company, and gave these two performances plus the premiere of Edward Solomon's *The Nautch Girl* in 2004.

Although there were other productions between 2000 and 2004, none of them were ever finished, usually because of low interest. The group's members constantly changed, and it hardly ever featured the same talent twice. The goal of the company was to present unfamiliar English operas for the entertainment of the community, but few understood my vision, and even fewer supported it. My inexperience in directing and education, combined with Rockford's long-established indifference toward light opera, made for a challenging combination. The talent that took an interest in the group would often get frustrated with the low musical standards and low attendance, and never participate again. Those who remained tended to be inexperienced themselves, and thus, unqualified for such difficult music. Royal English Opera was forced to close and reorganize in September 2004.

During this time, I completed his college education and rebuilt my company. In the fall of 2005, plans were announced to bring back the company as Rockford Operetta Party. The first production would be the Gilbert and Sullivan classic *Patience*, and production would begin in the summer of 2006. This time, the company would make an effort to appeal to public taste and raise the standards of performance. Despite quality talent, publicity, and a new approach to spreading the word, *Patience* failed to attract and the debut of the new company resembled a *success d'estime*. Undaunted, I prepared the 2007 production of a very obscure opera called *Jane Annie*.

The sole opera written by the authors of *Peter Pan* and *Sherlock Holmes* had its North American premiere with Rockford Operetta Party on October 19, 2007, at Central Christian Church. For the first time, I hit a home run in producing light opera. Local publicity was friendly, and the cast, though mostly of high school age, were quite skilled in bringing this neglected musical back to life. A new era of light opera was about to begin, but the 2008 production of my opera *Not So Good as La Traviata* was nothing like *Jane Annie*'s degree of quality. It was several steps back, due to an appalling cast, weak leadership, and an under-prepared orchestra. *Traviata* forced the company to close its doors again, and in 2009, no production was given. Word about the 2008 production got around fast, with the result that almost no one supported a light opera company in Rockford. The eagerly-anticipated series of quality opera programmes, it seemed, would not materialize after all.

But *ogni medaglia ha il suo reverso*! 2009 was not a wasted year for the group. I was busy behind the scenes, reorganizing and planning for a return in 2010, and with the support of my church and the pre-*Traviata* talent, the company was alive again, but not in Rockford. During a self-imposed exile in Winnebago, I gave my next three programmes at my church in that town. The first was on

March 11, 2010, and the company presented something called *Sunsets and Edelweiss*, a concert of Edwardian light opera. For the centenary of the last Savoy opera, *Two Merry Monarchs*, the Party performed selections from that opera and two other contemporary works: *A Welsh Sunset* and *The Mountaineers*.

This programme was a strong success, and featured some superb singing from Lorie Parker-Weinrich, Erica Reed, and Giovanni Grimaudo. Based on its success, the Party was nominated for a Mayor's Arts Award that autumn. In November, they presented Arthur Sullivan's opera *Cox and Box*, a more familiar opera that drew the talent of Elizabeth LaGrande O'Leary and established her as a mainstay of the company. At the close of 2010, they were invited to present *Cox and Box* at an international festival of the Gilbert and Sullivan operas. Another success was achieved by the Party in Andre Messager's *Mirette*, another North American premiere, on March 13, 2011.

Before the close of the year, Rockford Operetta Party was rumored to be returning to the Rockford stage in 2012. The original plans included a revival of *Not So Good as La Traviata*, but we decided to return with a different work instead. My librettist, John Spartan (a native of Long Island), and I wrote a new opera titled *Lindarella's List*, an original comic opera in one act. I composed the opera based on the talents of the Party, which featured many local performers.

This work had its world premiere on March 30, 2012 at the Mendelssohn Club on Church Street, and set the company a new attendance record. The audience seemed ready to seize on any excuse for enthusiasm, and applauded every song to the echo. Toward the end of the opera, the duet between myself and O'Leary was encored by the audience. Although only one performance was given, this opera re-established the company as a necessary fixture of the artistic community. In the autumn, they presented a concert of Gilbert and Sullivan. The Party were also the opening act for Rockford PrideFest in 2013, and in the fall of 2013, their *Edward German Revue* was performed.

At the time of writing this article, *HMS Pinafore* is in the works for the Party. Audiences recognize Rockford Operetta Party as an established light opera group that serves a specific niche audience. The Party is certainly not a household name, and our shows have not played to packed houses. We are, however, a struggling, yet innovative, nationally-recognized company that was established to present a unique art form in a unique manner. As Rome was not built in a day, neither was Rockford Operetta Party. Using local performers, the Party educates audiences and encourages individual participation, which heightens Rockford's artistic and cultural life.

Works Cited

"Works of area playwrights to hit Midway Village," *Register Star* (Rockford) 23 July 2000.

"Royal English Opera Holds Final Production," *Rock River Times* (Rockford) 30 July 2004.

"The WORST opera ever? Rockford Operetta Party stages notorious 'Jane Annie, or The Good Conduct Prize'," *Register Star* (Rockford) 16 October 2007.

"Rockford Operetta Party Presents 'Jane Annie'," *Daily Republica* (Belvidere) 14 October 2007.

"Rockford Operetta Party presents 'Sunsets and Edelweiss' March 11, 13," *Rock River Times* (Rockford) 10-16 March 2010.

State of the Arts Luncheon Programme, 6 October 2010.

Brochure for the International Gilbert and Sullivan Festival at Gettysburg 2011.

Farrell, Scott, "Letter to the editor," *Rockford Register Star* (Rockford) 18 March 2011.

"Rockford Operetta Party returns with comedic opera," *Register Star* (Rockford) 25 March 2012.

Rockford PrideFest Programme, 1-2 June 2013.

OUR GENERATION'S REVOLUTION IS TO REBEL AGAINST GREED

BRANDON REID

Greed. No other word better describes the ill of our society today. Greed is prevalent in politics, sports, Hollywood, the corporate world, the media, and even in our personal lives. Greed, particularly in media and politics, is the single-greatest threat to our democracy and the liberty it provides.

Particularly in the past decade, greed has played a major role in the erosion of the American press and the values to which it once subscribed. Within the world of politics, the influence of greed and wealth on our political system has alienated voters and co-opted our elected officials and Supreme Court justices.

In short, greed has taken away our freedom of speech and the liberty envisioned by our nation's founders.

How corporate media are destroying your liberty

Investors in the corporate media world have no interest in "reasonable profits"; they want massive profits. In fact, in the early to mid-2000s, corporate media owners and shareholders regularly sought profit margins of 15 to 20 percent. With a decline in readership, however, the overall average operating profit margin for newspapers in the United States is now around 11 percent. That number continues to fall as many large corporate media outlets struggle with massive debt and declining circulation. Circulation has dropped an average of 2 percent per year for many newspapers in the United States, and that number is now accelerating.

Stockholders and investors in media corporations from about the 1980s to the mid-2000s regularly demanded endless increases in profit margins. To do this, corporate media outlets laid off and outsourced staff, reduced news holes, and avoided writing anything controversial that would scare away advertisers and readers ("news holes" are the amount of space on a page in a newspaper or magazine dedicated to news content as opposed to advertising content). The result was a sleeping watchdog that allowed corruption and complacency in government to reign supreme.

With the watering down of our news, is it any wonder circulation at many newspapers has continued to decline? Many of these corporate media outlets are now in so deep financially that their only answer is more layoffs, more outsourcing, smaller news holes, and even less actual news coverage — all in desperate attempts to avoid bankruptcy. These efforts will likely only result in a further decline in circulation for many publications.

Some publications have not survived the perversion of stockholder greed. Notably, *The Rocky Mountain News* closed altogether, while *The Seattle Post-Intelligencer* reduced its operations to Internet-only. Many other publications — large and small — have followed the same path as both *The Rocky Mountain News* and *The Seattle Post-Intelligencer*, and a number of other large, financially troubled newspapers across the country are seeking buyers, including the local *Rockford Register Star*.

With regard to the quality of journalism offered today, the "old" tenets of accuracy, freedom of information, and the media as a watchdog of government are no longer attractive to the corporate media world. The main tenets of the "new" media are "IMMEDIACY! IMMEDIACY!! IMMEDIACY!!!" and "MONEY! MONEY!! MONEY!!!" The main tenets of the "old" media take a back seat, if they're even in the same vehicle.

The Internet, of course, has played a role in the changing face of journalism. No other information vehicle in history has been capable of delivering the news to its audience at such a high speed. This has led many newsrooms to put a greater emphasis on immediacy. Every media outlet wants to get the story NOW, so they can later brag about "having it first." Little concern is shown in being "the first to get it right."

Immediacy comes at a very high price because it often compromises a key tenet of "old" journalism — accuracy. When media deliver stories that are not accurate, they lose credibility with their audience, and the "new" corporate media's push for IMMEDIACY! over ACCURACY! has significantly damaged the longterm credibility of the media. If people do not view the media as credible, how effective can the media be in serving our democracy as watchdogs of government?

Furthermore, corporate media often come up short in their

role as watchdogs. A perfect example is the local daily, the *Rockford Register Star*, which was pretty much privately and/or locally held until about 1967 when The Gannett Company, based in McClean, Va., purchased the daily's founding publications the *Register Republic* and the *Rockford Morning Star*. Gannett merged the two papers into the *Rockford Register Star* in 1979.

As mentioned in a 2007 series in *The Rock River Times*, the *Register Star*'s lack of coverage as a watchdog of government during its years under corporate ownership has been detrimental to an already struggling Rockford community. Two examples given in that series were the daily's coverage of the school desegregation lawsuit in the late 1980s and early 1990s, and the coverage of the 1-percent sales tax increase that went to fund the Winnebago County Justice Center in 2002. The newspaper failed in both cases, in my opinion, to expose the corruption behind these issues or foretell their longterm ramifications.

Many other examples could be given, including the newspaper's resistance from 2009 to 2011 to expose the corrupt and unethical leadership of the Dr. LaVonne M. Sheffield administration in Rockford Public School District 205. Sheffield served as superintendent of the school district during that period, and many allegations were brought by students, teachers, and administrators. Not only were these allegations mostly ignored by the local daily, but the local daily's leadership largely supported Sheffield in many editorials and articles. In fact, the local daily held a number of "media round-tables" during this period to effectively tell other local media outlets how to properly cover the school district.

Sheffield ultimately announced her resignation in April 2011 following months of protests from teachers, staff, and students. The resignation also came after *The Rock River Times* was the only local media outlet to pursue under the Freedom of Information Act (FOIA) release of an unflattering letter written by former Rockford Auburn High School Principal and then-Freeport High School Principal Dr. Patrick Hardy. The letter included many disturbing details regarding Sheffield's leadership style. The Nov. 24, 2010, release of the letter came after four months of pursuit by *The Rock*

River Times that included multiple FOIA requests, a lawsuit filed against the district by *The Rock River Times* and the Illinois Press Association (IPA), a series of editorials, and the printing of other news articles about the matter. The local daily and other media outlets, meantime, essentially derided the weekly *Rock River Times* for having the audacity to challenge the school district.

However, on August 18, 2011, the IPA and *The Rock River Times* were declared victorious in Winnebago County court in a groundbreaking lawsuit against Rockford Public School District 205 and Sheffield over violations and abuse of the state's FOIA. The lawsuit, filed in November 2010 by the IPA and *The Rock River Times*, was the first case filed under Illinois' new FOIA, which went into effect Jan. 1, 2010. As a result of the lawsuit, the Winnebago County Circuit Court of the 17th Judicial Circuit imposed civil penalties against the school district in the amount of $2,500 for its repeated violations of FOIA involving one document. Despite the letter being deemed a public document by the Attorney General's Public Access Counselor, the school district had refused to release the letter on three separate occasions, citing two different FOIA exemptions. The school district even went as far as labeling the decision of the Attorney General's Office as "erroneous."

In his ruling, Winnebago County Circuit Judge Eugene G. Doherty, said, "The record gives a clear impression that the District understood that it was wrong on all three claimed exemptions, but was looking for a way to save face rather than simply admitting it was wrong and disclosing the document." He further states, "the entire course of events here strongly suggest that the District first decided that it would not release a document which it did not want to release, and only then did it begin looking for reasons to support a decision it had already made. The invocation of a new (and equally unfounded) basis for exemption after the first reasons had been proven incorrect is an indication of the District's intransigence. Only when the requesting party filed suit was the District finally compelled to concede that its position was indefensible."

In praising the ruling, Illinois Attorney General Lisa Madigan (D) said: "This case demonstrates the critical importance of enforceable transparency laws. People have a fundamental right to know how their government conducts itself on their behalf."

The IPA and *The Rock River Times* were represented by Don Craven of Springfield, legal counsel for the IPA. Craven said: "This case was a poster child for the imposition of civil penalties. The district was delaying, playing games and exemption shopping. When pushed, they invented a conversation with PAC Cara Smith—a conversation she says never took place—and released the document at 5 p.m. on Thanksgiving Eve, citing, of course, their long-standing policy of open and transparent government. Perhaps writing this check for civil penalties will encourage the district to have a slightly more sincere policy in support of open and transparent government."

The recent demise of the local daily

The daily was purchased April 12, 2007, by GateHouse Media, Inc., a corporation based in Fairport, N.Y., that is owned by hedge fund and venture capital firm Fortress Investment Group, LLC. The purchase was part of a $410 million deal that also included the GateHouse purchase of three other Gannett daily newspapers—the *Norwich* (Conn.) *Bulletin*, the *Observer-Dispatch* in Utica, New York, and *The Herald-Dispatch* in Huntington, West Virginia.

GateHouse publishes nearly 90 daily and 265 weekly newspapers and employs 4,565 people across 21 states. When GateHouse purchased the *Register Star* in 2007, the company's stock was trading at $21 per share. By 2008, the company had been delisted from the New York Stock Exchange.

In February 2012, in attempts to avoid bankruptcy, GateHouse announced plans to consolidate production of all of the company's publications to two main production centers in Rockford and Framingham, Massachusetts. Also around the same time, portions of the local daily's graphics and advertising design departments were outsourced to India and other locations in the United States. Then, May 13, 2013, GateHouse announced it was scrapping the February 2012 plans and would consolidate production of its publications to one central production hub. That location had yet to be announced, but GateHouse said the new center would "not be based in an existing GateHouse Media facility."

On Sept. 3, 2013, despite its struggles, GateHouse Media acquired management of an additional eight daily newspapers and 15 weekly newspapers in seven states. The daily newspapers included the *Ashland Daily Tidings* in Oregon; *Cape Cod Times* of Barnstable, Mass.; *Mail Tribune* of Oregon; *Pocono Record* of Stroudsburg, Pa.; *The Portsmouth Herald* of Portsmouth, N.H.; *The Record* of Stockton, Calif.; *The Standard-Times* of New Bedford, Mass.; and *Times Herald-Record* of Middletown, N.Y.

On Sept. 11, 2013, GateHouse filed for bankruptcy.

Not that the *Register Star* is fully responsible for all that has happened—good or bad—in Rockford since 1979, but it has played a part, either through its coverage or lack of coverage. It has done some good, but many readers have noticed over the years how the paper keeps getting thinner and thinner, how more and more space is being devoted to "canned" news and shorter stories, and how the paper is producing as many products as possible in attempts to make more money. Are these products really aimed at helping keep us informed as civic-minded participants in democracy, or are they aimed at simply using us as consumers?

In the past decade, poverty within the city of Rockford has more than doubled, while the unemployment rate has remained above 10 percent for the past five years. The violent crime rate is among the highest in the country, crumbling roads continue to crisscross the city, and the high school dropout rate has led Rockford's public schools to become known as "dropout factories."

Corruption, cronyism, and greed have all contributed to the "misery" of Rockford. Unfortunately, those who own shares in and those who run the daily's parent company—and ultimately dictate what the daily does—don't care about Rockford's misery. Many of them would probably even struggle to find Rockford on a map—of northern Illinois.

Daily newspaper circulation has been on the decline since the 1980s, when the large-scale buyout of our freedom of speech began. People have already begun to turn to non-corporate and locally-owned media and the Internet. But the question we have to ask ourselves is, in a democracy, should our media's No. 1 goal be to make money, or to hold public officials accountable for their actions and expose corruption and complacency in government?

As Thomas Jefferson said, "Our liberty depends on the freedom of the press, and that cannot be limited without being lost."

By buying gobs of newspapers and other media at a time, cutting and slashing them down to the bare minimum of quality for "efficiency" purposes, and using them simply as money-making tools for their stockholders, corporations have taken away the voice of the people. Corporate greed *has* limited the freedom of the press.

In the words of Jefferson, "Every generation needs a new revolution." The revolution of this generation should be to rebel against greed.

Join the revolution against greed in corporate media. For those with the means and the desire, donate money to a department of journalism and tell them to use the money only for programs that support civic-minded journalism. For those planning a career in journalism, only send your résumés to non-corporate and locally-owned media. If you're a reader, stop your subscription to corporately-owned media; read, watch, listen, log on to and subscribe to non-corporate and locally-owned media. If you're an advertiser, stop your advertisements with corporately-owned media and advertise with non-corporate and locally-owned media. If you're a consumer, which we all are, support businesses that advertise in non-corporate and locally-owned media, and tell businesses that don't advertise in non-corporate and locally-owned media to advertise in non-corporate and locally-owned media.

Our democracy—and your liberty—depend on your interest in how our media operate. Support non-corporate and locally-owned media and the schools that train those who will someday run the media. That's the only hope we have of regaining our freedom of the press and preserving the liberty it provides.

That's the bottom line.

Journalists trained to watch bottom line, not government

Greed has played a role in journalism schools across the country, as they have largely conformed to the tenets of the "new" corporate media world. The transformation is a trickle-down result of corporate media giving readers what they want, and journalism schools giving the corporate media what they want—a journalist trained to the bottom line.

Corporate media want to hire journalists who are trained in "bottom-line journalism"—or journalism that costs little to produce and gives readers only what they *want* instead of information readers *need* to be informed citizens. These changes in the role of journalists in our society are already having significant impacts on our democracy.

Journalism schools across the country have shown a tendency in recent years to put a greater emphasis on training journalists the basics of writing and editing and on advertising and business, while putting less emphasis on teaching journalists the importance of the First Amendment and the role of journalists as watchdogs of government.

Many schools have changed their curriculum requirements to involve more business-minded courses as opposed to civic-minded courses. The journalism curriculum itself seems to focus more on "immediacy," which provides surface-level reporting, as opposed to accuracy and investigation, which provide in-depth reporting.

Two journalism departments from which I graduated—the undergraduate program at Drake University in Des Moines, Iowa, and the graduate program at the University of Illinois at Urbana-Champaign—continue to try to balance the tenets of the "new" corporate media with the "old" tenets of civic-minded journalism. However, changes to curriculum within both of these schools in the past decade have leaned more toward the tenets of the "new" corporate media world.

I graduated from Drake University's undergraduate journalism program in 2001. Through that point, the school was guided by the wisdom of two old-school journalists (and great teachers)—Herb Strentz and Bob Woodward (not *that* Bob Woodward, but "the other Bob Woodward"). Strentz went into partial retirement that year, while Woodward retired in 2004.

I remember one time working late at the campus newspaper at Drake in 2000. The newspaper's office was in the same building as the offices of journalism professors. I was alone in the newspaper office, when Woodward—with light gray beard and light gray hair combed over his head and down the side of his face in one of the most eccentric and carefully-crafted comb-overs in history—shuffled in the door and sat down in a chair next to me. He looked exhausted, and began talking about the politics behind the College of Communications and how much of a struggle it was to fight for the Department of Journalism. At the time, the college was considering cutting all funding to the campus newspaper, and making significant changes to the curriculum.

Woodward, who always said journalists needed to have a certain "energy," always displayed that energy himself every time he was around students. That energy was not present that night in the newspaper office. He looked dejected and deflated. He retired four years later, after the new curriculum went into effect.

Woodward was a phenomenal teacher. He was a former principal assistant national editor and world editor at *The Washington* (D.C.) *Star* from 1965 to 1972 (the evening newspaper in Washington, D.C.). He was at John F. Kennedy's funeral. His main tenet was "ACCURACY! ACCURACY!! ACCURACY!!!" and he insisted on being fair and balanced, and "getting the list and following the money."

Strentz was all about the First Amendment and freedom of information. In fact, he often would joke that he started each day on the hill in his back yard screaming at the top of his lungs, "FREEDOM OF INFORMATION! FREEDOM OF INFORMATION!! FREEDOM OF INFORMATION!!!" He was secretary and founding member of the Iowa Freedom of Information Council (IFIC). His unforgettable quote to our class regarding obscenity in journalism was, "I have no problem with shit, piss, or tits."

More eloquently is the quote from James Madison often quoted by the IFIC: "Knowledge will forever govern ignorance. And a people who mean to be their own governors must arm themselves with the power knowledge gives. A popular government without popular information or the means of acquiring it is but a prologue to a farce or a tragedy, or perhaps both."

At the University of Illinois, my uncle, the late Bob Reid, was referred to by his colleagues as "the conscience of the college." He taught students that public affairs journalism was not just about a bunch of talking heads—but about people and how public policy affected their lives.

Reid encouraged students to be "Curious Georges" who would ask endless questions and want to know everything about everything. Instead of teaching classes about "how to write the perfect lead" or "how to construct the perfect story in inverted pyramid format," his classes focused on what to do when you have to decide—on deadline—whether to use a picture of a person jumping to his death from near the top of the World Trade Center on 9/11 or whether it's ethical for a journalist to accept financial support from a public figure.

He wanted to make people think, and—above all—emphasized the important role journalists play in our democracy.

As Reid, himself a product of the "old" civic-minded Medill School of Journalism, wrote in a column titled "Are profits killing newspapers?" for the U of I Department of Journalism's online magazine *Spike* in January 2000:

"In a very real sense, newspapers have been, are and will remain the day-to-day textbooks of our democracy. Newspapers can provide us with accurate views of the world outside our immediate, personal gaze. Those views—or the lack of them—shape our agendas and actions as citizens. If newspapers lose their credibility with the public through a loss of belief that they are trying to tell the truth, fairly and responsibly, then citizens are left to grope largely in the dark.

"Quite rightly, those who control newspapers worry about the effect of rising public skepticism. But they tend to worry more about this as a matter of losing potential profits than as one of losing the potential to better inform citizens. Thus, the response of many of these newspaper executives has been to apply modern management techniques to the running of their newsrooms. These techniques generally are generic ones, devised so that those who learn them can run a soap factory or a department store profitably. Such techniques stress employing market studies, enforcing uniform production methods, cutting costs and using a variety of equivalents to the assembly-line production of goods and services. The techniques apply well to some aspects of what newspapers do, but poorly to others. ...

"Although newspaper profits in general are very high compared with other businesses, many newspaper customers are receiving a lower quality and are paying a higher price for what they get currently versus previously. Profits have been kept at high levels by considerable cost-cutting, including areas of newspaper operations where the quality, ethics and morals of journalistic performance are at stake. This has seriously diminished the ability of many newspapers to fulfill their roles as civic educators and civic watchdogs.

"Expensive, serious reporting has become less frequent, cheaper fluff and sensationalism more prevalent. In many instances, senior editors are so engaged in marketing and other management activities that they no longer closely review major stories before publication or even spend much time with their sub-editors and reporters.

"Around the country, many papers are no longer attracting as many of the best and brightest from the next generation as they once did. Also, cost-cutting has forced some of the best of seasoned, serious journalists into early retirement.

"Making profit the main goal of journalistic endeavor has demoralized many of the best reporters and editors. This has led a few of the more ambitious or more insecure journalists into some serious ethical lapses that have resulted in fabricated, sensational or under-reported stories. With increasingly large portions of the literate public, all of this has seriously undercut the credibility of newspapers. That, in turn, has led to calls from powerful people in business, politics and the judiciary for shrinking First Amendment rights.

"I think it's time for newspaper publishers to consider the prudence of using these thoroughly modern management practices so single-mindedly. ..."

After reviewing some of his personal experiences from his newspaper career that proved responsible journalism could deliver what he called "reasonable profits," his column concluded:

"High-quality journalism, in short, is both practical and good for the ideals our society cherishes most. The core problems of newspapers today are not ones of systemic inevitability. Rather, newspapers face a challenge relating to human character: a challenge to their publishers, editors and reporters to act with real respect for readers and potential readers—as have John Gardner, Gene Roberts, and Nelson Poynter along with the Sulzberger family in New York, the Grahams in Washington, D.C., and the owners of *The Wall Street Journal*.

"All of them have proved that individual profiles in courage are not incompatible with realizing reasonable profits. They also have demonstrated that reasonable profits are not incompatible with conducting responsible and ethical journalism. That is the only kind of journalism capable of commanding the respect which ultimately is vital to preserving the freedoms our society enjoys under the First Amendment to the constitution for the children and grandchildren who follow us. Future generations depend on us to be responsible stewards of the freedoms we have been given, freedoms we should strive to hand down to them intact. We owe them nothing less."

The only problem is, corporate media have not been interested in "reasonable profits"; they have wanted massive profits. And corporate media believe they will not get massive profits by continuing to use the traditional tenets of journalism. Instead, they prefer media that are more reactive—giving audiences only what they want—than proactive—giving audiences what they need to know to be informed citizens in our democracy.

The impact of this on journalism schools is a change in their curriculum away from civic-minded journalism and toward bottom-line journalism.

Publicly-funded campaigns only hope of saving 'government of the people'

While greed has certainly had a profound impact on our media, it has also had a very powerful impact on our government. Jan. 14, 2007, the voice of the people was overpowered by the snorting, grunting hog farm of corporate greed. On that date, Rockford City Council voted 8-5 in support of Rockford Blacktop's proposed special-use permit, which allowed the company to construct and operate a hot-mix asphalt plant on the floor of its Mulford Quarry.

The approval of the permit came despite months of protest by neighbors of the quarry, 350 of whom organized as the Neighborhood Environment and Traffic Safety group, which reportedly had a support base of about 3,000. Those neighbors were concerned about contaminants in the water and air, noise, traffic congestion, and decreased home values.

By voting for the proposed special-use permit, eight aldermen proved their political souls had been sold to corporate greed. Apparently, the group of eight aldermen who voted for the special-use permit were more persuaded by the power of the dollar than by the power of the people—an all-too-common occurrence in our democracy.

Rockford Blacktop—and its parent company, William Charles, Ltd.—at the time of the 2007 vote, were among the most influential local financial contributors to politicians, political parties, and political action groups. The Illinois State Board of Elections' Campaign Disclosure website at *www.elections.il.gov* showed that, as of Oct. 12, 2007, William Charles, Ltd., had contributed $135,999.35 to 134 recipients and Rockford Blacktop had contributed $64,218.88 to 52 recipients.

Additionally, the same website showed individuals associated with William Charles, Ltd., and Rockford Blacktop were also heavy contributors. As of Oct. 12, 2007, Gary Marzorati, president of

William Charles Waste Companies, had donated $13,442.29 to 37 recipients; Neil Maloney, a consultant for William Charles Investments, had donated $6,000 to seven recipients; Charles Uram, insurance administrator for William Charles, Ltd., had donated $3,150 to 11 recipients; and Charles Howard, president of Rockford Blacktop, had donated $2,100 to three recipients.

All told, Rockford Blacktop, William Charles, Ltd., and the individuals associated with the company had donated at least $224,910.52 to political causes. Apparently, that amount of money was more powerful than the collective voice of 3,000 people in the city council's Jan. 14, 2007, asphalt plant vote.

Worth noting is that the perversion of greed continues to have an impact on local politics. In the 2013 race for Rockford mayor, incumbent Larry Morrissey (I) raised more than $50,000, Democratic challenger Jim Hughes raised more than $35,000 and Republican challenger Michael Kleen raised more than $1,200 in individual contributions and loaned his own campaign $1,514.73. The power of the dollar once again paid off for Morrissey, as he won a third term behind 44 percent of the vote (8,424 votes). Hughes had 38 percent (7,196 votes) and Kleen 18 percent (3,502 votes) in that election.

First Rockford Group Founder and President Sunil Puri and Joseph Behr & Sons, Inc., were among notable A-1 contributors to Morrissey's campaign. Puri donated $1,001 to Morrissey's campaign March 7, 2013, and Joseph Behr & Sons donated $6,000 to Morrissey's campaign in contributions made Dec. 10, 2012, and Dec. 28, 2012. The Illinois State Board of Elections' campaign disclosure website also showed SupplyCore, Inc., has given more than $150,000 in contributions, in-kind donations, services and loans to Morrissey's campaign since 2001. Morrissey's most recent D-2 quarterly report of contributions indicated his campaign, "Citizens for Morrissey," owed a total of $28,700 in debt to SupplyCore, Inc. The debt was in relation to loans given April 1, 2005 (original amount was $20,000) and May 23, 2005 (original amount was $13,500). Citizens for Morrissey has paid a total of $4,800 toward the debt.

172

In the meantime, Hughes accepted two donations—totaling $4,505—from retired Winnebago County Sheriff Donald Gasparini in the 2013 mayoral election cycle. Gasparini was at the center of a controversy in 2011 when the Winnebago County Forest Preserve District (WCFPD) purchased 18 acres of land from the former sheriff for $216,500. The land was adjacent to the Four Lakes Forest Preserve near Pecatonica, Ill., and included three fishing ponds. The $216,500 price tag was set by private appraiser Harrison & Associates, Inc., of Woodstock, Ill. That same company appraised the land at $248,000 in 2004. Although the WCFPD purchased the land at a price set by a private appraiser, the deal led many to believe cronyism was involved, as Gasparini was longtime friends with then-WCFPD Board President Randy Olson.

In August 2012, Olson was stripped of his position after commissioners voted to remove him from the president's chair. Olson had created a new public safety and risk management job without the board's consent and had handpicked Theresa Rawaillot, a 13-year Roscoe police veteran and his fellow Law Enforcement Aviation Coalition member, to fill the position.

Voice of the people not being heard

The overwhelming impact of greed on our government is that the voice the people is not being heard.

One person who understood the importance of the voice of the people in our democracy was our 16th president, Abraham Lincoln. As Lincoln said in his Gettysburg Address Nov. 19, 1863, at the dedication of the Soldiers' National Cemetery in Gettysburg, Pa.:

"Four score and seven years ago our fathers brought forth on this continent a new nation, conceived in Liberty, and dedicated to the proposition that all men are created equal.

"Now we are engaged in a great civil war, testing whether that nation, or any nation, so conceived and so dedicated, can long endure. We are met on a great battle-field of that war. We have come to dedicate a portion of that field, as a final resting place for those who here gave their lives that that nation might live. It is altogether fitting and proper that we should do this.

"But, in a larger sense, we can not dedicate—we can not consecrate—we can not hallow—this ground. The brave men, living and dead, who struggled here, have consecrated it, far above our poor power to add or detract. The world will little note, nor long remember what we say here, but it can never forget what they did here. It is for us the living, rather, to be dedicated here to the unfinished work which they who fought here have thus far so nobly advanced. It is rather for us to be here dedicated to the great task remaining before us—that from these honored dead we take increased devotion to that cause for which they gave the last full measure of devotion—that we here highly resolve that these dead shall not have died in vain—that this nation, under God, shall have a new birth of freedom—and that government of the people, by the people, for the people, shall not perish from the earth."

Furthermore, the basis for the main principles of our democracy of which Lincoln spoke came from the Declaration of Independence, whose principal author—Thomas Jefferson—would serve as the third president of our nation. As the Declaration of Independence, adopted July 4, 1776, states:

"We hold these truths to be self-evident, that all men are created equal, that they are endowed by their Creator with certain unalienable Rights, that among these are Life, Liberty, and the pursuit of Happiness.

"That to secure these rights, Governments are instituted among Men, deriving their just powers from the consent of the governed, That whenever any Form of Government becomes destructive of these ends, it is the Right of the People to alter or abolish it, and to institute new Government, laying its foundation on such principles and organizing its powers in such form, as to them shall seem most likely to effect their Safety and Happiness. Prudence, indeed, will dictate that Governments long established should not be changed for light and transient causes; and accordingly all experience hath shewn, that mankind are more disposed to suffer, while evils are sufferable, than to right themselves by abolishing the forms to which they are accustomed. But when a long train of abuses and usurpations, pursuing invariably the same Object evinces a design to reduce them under absolute Despotism, it is their right, it is their duty, to throw off such Government, and to provide new Guards for their future security."

Every man and woman registered to vote is entitled to the equal right to vote. And regardless of income or the number and amount of political contributions made, every individual registered to vote has one vote equal to the vote of every other registered man and woman. As the Declaration of Independence states, "Governments are instituted among Men, deriving their powers from the consent of the governed" to "secure" our rights to "Life, Liberty, and the pursuit of Happiness."

However, those who have the means to contribute to political campaigns and the desire to influence elected officials—the wealthy and the greedy—are the ones who determine who can and who cannot run for public office and what legislation is presented and passed. As a result, the wealthy and the greedy—particularly in Rockford—set the agenda, and, ultimately, dictate what course our government takes by using their influence to get what they want. Such was the case in the Rockford City Council's 2007 approval of Rockford Blacktop's special-use permit for the asphalt plant, and such was the case in the 2013 Rockford mayoral election.

How can we have a nation of liberty, "dedicated to the proposition that all men are created equal," as Lincoln said, when that proposition is perverted by the influence of wealth and greed? All men do not have equal political spending power—and all men certainly do not have equal political spending power in relation to corporations.

Locally, at the time of the city council's vote on the asphalt plant in 2007, AMCORE Bank (now BMO Harris Bank) had donated $278,133.60 to 287 political recipients and Sunil Puri of First Rockford Group had donated $320,558.12 to 94 political recipients. At the time of the 2000 Census, the median Rockford income was $37,098 for men and $25,421 for women. That means it would take the average Rockford man about seven-and-a-half years—without spending a penny of his income—to save as much as AMCORE Bank had donated to political causes, and it would take the average Rockford woman about 11 years to do the same. Similarly, it would take the average Rockford man a little more than eight-and-a-half years—without spending a penny of his income—to save as much as Puri had donated to political causes, and it would take the average Rockford woman a little more than 12 years to do the same.

One-hundred-fifty years after Lincoln delivered the Gettysburg Address, the time has come for us to honor the 620,000 who lost their lives fighting for a "government of the people, by the people, for the people"—and not a "government of the dollar, by the dollar, for the dollar." The time has come for us to put the power of our democracy back in the hands of the people—and free it from the constraints of the wealthy and the greedy. For as sure as the oppressive chains of slavery were a cancer on the "unalienable Rights" of "Life, Liberty, and the pursuit of Happiness," so, too, are the oppressive chains of wealth and greed and their influence on our democracy.

Clean elections one way to break free of the effects of greed

One way some states and local jurisdictions have broken free of the constraints of the wealthy and the greedy is to use what are referred to as "clean elections"—or "clean money"/"voter-owned elections." Under this system of campaign financing, candidates who want to receive public financing collect a required number of small "qualifying contributions" from voters. These contributions are usually around $5. The candidates must also promise not to raise money from private sources. In return, those candidates who qualify for public funding are paid an equal flat sum by the government to finance their campaigns. Those who are outspent by other privately-funded candidates often receive additional public matching funds.

According to a report by PQ Media, "Political campaign spending on advertising media and marketing services is expected to rocket to an all-time high of $4.5 billion in the 2008 election cycle, driven by an acrimonious political environment, record fund-raising and the high number of presidential candidates." The report added this "is expected to be 43.3 percent more than in the 2006 cycle and is projected to soar 64.1 over the 2004 election cycle, the previous presidential campaign year." And that $4.5 billion is just the money that was spent on advertising and marketing; it didn't include other campaign costs. The total for the 2012 election cycle, meantime, was yet another new record—$6 billion.

Instead of pouring all of this money into political campaigns, imagine if we had publicly-funded campaigns and everyone kept their money and instead spent it on deserving nonprofit groups, consumer goods and services, or other investments, including stocks and bonds. How much stronger could our economy be with that $6 billion alone, even if we each had to pay about $1 per year on taxes to fund political campaigns?

While many politicians have pushed for caps on political contributions, in 1976—ironically our nation's bicentennial year—the United States Supreme Court ruled in *Buckley v. Valeo* that spending money to influence elections is a form of constitutionally protected free speech. And then, in 2010, in *Citizens United v. Federal Election Commission*, the U.S. Supreme Court unleashed a flood of corporate money into our political system by ruling that, contrary to longstanding precedents, corporations have a First Amendment right to spend unlimited amounts of money to promote or defeat candidates. The decision overturned a century of campaign finance law and led to record spending by outside groups and super PACs in the 2012 elections (hence the record $6 billion price tag). As of September 2013, 16 states had formally called for an amendment by ballot measure, resolutions passed by the legislature, or official letters signed by a majority of state legislators in opposition to the *Citizens United* ruling. Those states were California, Colorado, Connecticut, Delaware, Hawaii, Illinois, Maine, Maryland, Massachusetts, Montana, New Jersey, New Mexico, Oregon, Rhode Island, Vermont and West Virginia.

In addition, nearly 500 cities, towns and counties, including New York, Los Angeles, Chicago, and Philadelphia, have called for an amendment, and more than 2,000 elected officials nationwide are on record supporting one. A 2010 Peter Hart poll found 82 percent of

Americans supported congressional action to limit corporate spending on elections (which *Citizens United* unleashed), and that 79 percent supported a constitutional amendment to accomplish this. A September 2013 Associated Press poll found that 83 percent of Americans favor limits on the amount of money corporations, unions, and other organizations can spend on elections. The 2012 AP poll also showed that 81 percent of Republicans, 78 percent of independents, and 85 percent of Democrats wanted to limit corporate, union, and other outside spending.

Going even beyond the *Citizens United* ruling, the U.S. Supreme Court is also hearing arguments in the case of *McCutcheon v. Federal Election Commission*, which would challenge overall contribution limits for individual donors that were first enacted in the mid-1970s. The case has been dubbed "*Citizens United*, Round 2." A ruling in favor of McCutcheon would end the $117,000 cap on contributions and allow unlimited contributions from individuals.

Should there be a price tag on 'free speech'?

What's somewhat surprising is the United States Supreme Court would find monetary political contributions to be free speech. How is speech that costs $320,558 (for example) free? There should be no price tag on free speech, particularly when it applies to essential democratic discourse.

Free speech is speech afforded to everyone; bought speech is afforded only to those who can afford to buy it. When bought speech is viewed as being the same as free speech, it does not uphold equality, and it does not allow for "Life, Liberty, and the pursuit of Happiness."

In dissent of *Buckley*, Supreme Court Justice Byron White "argued that the entire law should have been upheld, in deference to Congress's greater knowledge and expertise on the issue." Some Supreme Court justices, notably Clarence Thomas and Antonin Scalia (neither of whom was on the court at the time of *Buckley*), have argued for overturning *Buckley* on these grounds, but their position has not been adopted by the court.

Just as we needed an amendment to the Constitution to break free of the oppressive chains of slavery, so, too, do we need an amendment to the Constitution to break free of the oppressive chains of wealth and greed and their influence on our democracy. We need an amendment to the Constitution that makes the current system of privately-funded campaigns unconstitutional, and puts the power of our democracy back where it belongs—in the voice of the people and their right to vote. One vote for every registered man or woman—free of the perversion of greed and wealth—is true equality that leads to true liberty. Such an amendment is the only hope we have of ensuring our nation—"conceived in Liberty, and dedicated to the proposition that all men are created equal"—long endures.

JUST AN ORDINARY DAY

THE STORY OF LAURETTA LYONS

KATHI KRESOL

Home of Mrs. Lauretta Lyons, murder victim
. . . Body found in pool of blood on living room floor

Register-Republic photo, 1966

"The life of the dead is placed in the memory of the living."
—Marcus Tillius Cicero

L ooking back, June 9, 1966 started out as just another typical day. The weather was overcast with an occasional drizzle. As Edwin Lyons and his wife Lauretta had breakfast together before he left for work, there was nothing to indicate that day would be different from any other.

Edwin and Lauretta had been married in Dubuque, Iowa on October 20, 1939, when Lauretta was only 20-years-old. She had been born and raised in Rockford, and it was here that they decided to make their home. Both Lauretta and Edwin were considered successful. Lauretta had been a secretary at Block and Kuhl Department Store, but quit to open her own pet accessory store. Edwin and Lauretta were partners in this venture. They had a little shop on Mulberry Street in downtown Rockford called the Lyon's Den. They also traveled to fairs to display and sell the fancy dog collars from their shop.

Lauretta was a member of the Emmanuel Episcopal Church, the Rockford Women's Club, and the Rockford chapter of the Order of the Eastern Star. She was also a member of the American Kennel Club and the Canadian Club. Previously, she had been a member of the Business and Professional Women's Association. She also volunteered as a pink lady at Rockford Memorial Hospital gift shop.

Edwin worked as a chemist at the Rockford Drop Forge Company. Edwin's father was well known in Rockford. He owned the Brown's Business College. Edwin and Lauretta had operated the school for a while before it was sold in 1942. The school would eventually become the Rockford School of Business.

Edwin left home shortly after breakfast, right around 7:30am. The Lyons' house was a little off the beaten path, near where Latham Road intersects with Owen Center. It sat back a little ways from the road and was surrounded by trees and cornfields. It was not visible to any of the other houses. Later, when they were interviewed by the press, the Lyons' neighbors claimed that they did not know them very well. Richard T. Hare stated that he very rarely saw them.

Before Edwin left, he and Lauretta made plans for lunch. He was going to meet her at the shop. When Edwin left for work, he had no way of knowing that this seemingly ordinary day would turn out to be anything but that.

Lauretta was last seen by Julian Cwyman, a 38-year-old telephone repairman. He told deputies that he saw Lauretta with her three dogs walking around her yard. They had spoken briefly, and Lauretta even showed Cwyman some of the tricks she had taught the dogs. He left the area around 9:20am.

Edwin went to the shop for his lunch date with his wife, and he was surprised when she wasn't there. He tried to call her at home but received no answer, so he decided he better check on her to make sure everything was well.

He arrived home around 12:30pm. Edwin noticed that the doors were locked and the dogs were all inside. He walked into the living room and saw his wife lying on her stomach on the floor in a pool of blood. There were several of his neckties around her. One was even clenched in her hand.

He immediately called the Winnebago County Sheriff's Department and an ambulance. In the long moments it took help to arrive, he desperately searched for a pulse. Lauretta's favorite dog was curled up next to her and Edwin had to pick him up to get close to her. He noticed that its fur was still damp from an earlier walk.

Help finally arrived, but even though Edwin pleaded with the ambulance crew to, "Save her! Save her!" there was nothing to be done. They loaded Lauretta in the ambulance and drove her to Rockford Memorial Hospital where she was pronounced dead.

Sheriff's deputies arrived in full force. Lieutenant Michael Iasparro oversaw the investigation. They quickly noticed that all the doors were locked and that nothing was taken, even though there was a large amount of money in the home and a valuable stamp collection.

There were signs of a struggle. Furniture had been disturbed, a curtain was ripped down, and there was blood on the floor by the front door. This told investigators that Lauretta had fought her attacker. When Winnebago County Coroner Carl Sundberg conducted the autopsy on Lauretta, he reported that her jaw was swollen and that her lips and tongue were cut. She had not been raped, but she had been brutally strangled with one of her husband's neckties. The tie had gouged into her neck. Lauretta had another tie in her right hand and police discovered it had been cut off cleanly, apparently with scissors. They searched the entire house looking for the missing tip. It was never located.

Police theorized that someone might have come into the house while Lauretta was out walking her dogs and was waiting there when she returned. They fought in the living room and Lauretta broke free and made it to the door. She was then strangled from behind and left on the floor for hours until her husband found her.

Neighbors were questioned. Edwin was also interrogated, but his alibi held up. He told investigators that he had pulled his wife's car out of the garage for her before he left for work at 7:30am. Sheriff Kirk King was surprised when five people came forward to state that while they were driving past the home the morning of the murder, they had seen another car in the Lyons' driveway. It was described as a maroon 1957 Ford.

This case was never solved, but it may have been connected to another crime. A few weeks after the murder, there was another attack on a Rockford woman.

Charlene O'Brien had finished her shopping at the Colonial Village Mall and walked back to her car. The busy housewife and mother of three was confused when she tried to start her car and nothing happened. She must have felt a sense of relief when a man stepped forward to help. Rockford was a different place back in 1966, and Charlene probably felt no apprehension about accepting the help this man offered. It was a decision she would live to regret.

That man was no Good Samaritan. He had watched Charlene pull into the parking lot. He calmly strolled over to the car after she went in to do her shopping, lifted the hood, and tampered with the engine.

Then he calmly walked back over to the shadows to wait for Charlene to return. It was then that 43-year-old Sanford Harris stepped out of the dark, hiding his true nature as he slid into Charlene's vehicle. Only when he was inside of the car did the man strike. He knocked Charlene unconscious with a ball peen hammer.

Charlene was found 40 hours later, brutally beaten and abandoned along a farmer's lane near Perryville Road. Charlene was able to describe her attacker as a middle aged African American man and police quickly picked up Harris.

Harris was living with his common law wife, Mary Ann Walker. Walker told police she was 21 but they found out later she was only 15-years-old. He was on parole from the state of Michigan. Harris had killed a 41-year-old woman and received a life sentence, but won early release.

Sanford Harris was tried and convicted of the attack on Charlene O'Brien. He was sentenced to two concurrent terms of 75 to 90 years. According to the Rockford *Morning Star*, the judge who sentenced him called the attack, "The most sadistic and brutal attack he had ever witnessed."

People in Rockford were frightened after these two vicious attacks. The guns shops in town claimed that they sold three times the regular number of guns in the two week period following the attacks. People who had never locked their doors were buying extra locks.

Witnesses came forward to say that Harris' car looked very much like the car they had seen in front of Lauretta's house the day she was killed. Some of them were brought in for a line up and identified him as being the one they saw driving in the neighborhood that day. But police found no further hard evidence to place Harris at the scene. All of the items they had sent to the FBI came back negative. Charges were never filed against Harris for the murder of Lauretta.

The last newspaper article about Sanford Harris was written in June, 1983. It mentioned that he came up for parole every year since 1976. It also mentioned that the Winnebago County State's Attorney and the O'Brien family attended each and every hearing to give the testimony that they hoped would keep Harris behind bars.

Laureeta's story has made the newspaper several times, always as one of the unsolved crimes of this city. According to an article written in the Rockford *Register Star* in 2007, Rockford had formed a new cold case squad and Deputy Chief Dominic Iasparro mentioned that he hoped that they would look at the Lyons' case. Iasparro told of a special tie to Lauretta's case. Lt. Michael Iasparro was his father. Dominic Iasparro told the press, "There was significant focus on one suspect but there never enough evidence to charge that one individual."

It has been 47 years since Lauretta Lyons was killed in her own home. Almost as much time has passed since her death as she was on this earth. The chances are very slim now that her killer will ever be brought to justice. Her family must feel a little comfort that she has not been forgotten. It must bring them a little peace that the torch has been passed from the original officer to his son, who has now made it his mission to solve this horrible crime.

Works Cited

"Find Woman Bludgeoned to death in home here," *Register-Republic* (Rockford) Thursday, June 9, 1966.

"Neighbors: Lyons kept to themselves," *Register-Republic* (Rockford) Friday, June 10, 1966.

"Woman Found Murdered here," *Morning Star* (Rockford) Friday, June 10, 1966.

"Repairman last to see murder victim alive," *Register-Republic* (Rockford) Friday, June 10, 1966.

"Find Tracks at murder scene," *Morning Star* (Rockford) Saturday, June 11, 1966.

Obituary: "Lyons, Lauretta." *Morning Star* (Rockford) Sunday, June 12, 1966.

"Deputies Hunt maroon car in strangulation murder," *Morning Star* (Rockford) Wednesday, June 15, 1966.

"Harris linked to murder scene," *Morning Star* (Rockford) Wednesday, June 29, 1966.

"Report negative in Lyon's murder," *Morning Star* (Rockford) Sunday, August 21, 1966.

"Cold case to see some warmth," *Register Star* (Rockford) Sunday, March 11, 2007.

This photo of Mrs. Lauretta Lyons, found murdered Thursday in her home, was taken in January when Mrs. Lyons showed her dogs at a March of Dimes benefit. (Register-Republic staff photo)

Sanford N. Harris
. . . Trial will be held in Winnebago County

Register-Republic photos, 1966

LIFE, POVERTY, AND BASKETBALL

DAN CREVISTON

Life, Poverty, and Basketball

In my early pre-teen years, I became aware of the pain and broken promises other children like me endured in my hometown. A city full of suffering and neglect of its poor cast a great shadow over my heart while my mind slowly began to grasp the true meaning of what life *should* be. It only took one moment for me to understand the complexity of our issues. It would not be until I reached my twenties, however, that I realized how much of those issues are still molding the minds of our youth today. Our experiences steer us towards who we are, but it is the *perception* of those experiences that create and form us. We don't ask to be born in a certain place, to certain people, at a certain time. But when you are born into a place like Rockford, Illinois, you realize that someone must have done something horribly wrong to bring such falsity to your own being.

I grew up on Rockford's west side, near the corners of School Street and Avon. My passion during the first decade of my life was basketball. My neighbors were the only ones near me with a basketball hoop, so every single day I would be out there shooting around. It was a gravel court, which meant I quickly sharpened my handling skills and reflexes due to the amount of times the ball would bounce off a rock and go in an unintended direction. The fact that the neighbor kids were much older than I was mixed in with the complexity of the court. It was only natural that during those years I progressed to a point where I actually thought I might make the NBA. It was a young boy's dream, of course. Can you guess who my idol was? Yes, it was THAT guy. Due to the teenage pressures of life, however, I would never even play on a high school team.

The neighborhood I lived in, which was only a few blocks from the Fairgrounds housing complex, was a tough one for any child to grow up in. My father tells me that at a very young age I had learned to dive under a table when the sound of gunfire erupted. My mother and little brother were once chased by a group of kids who thought he was someone that they wanted to harm. I used to sit in the backyard and watch on-foot police chases through the woods towards Page Park. This was quite a frequent occurrence, given that poverty can escalate the aggressiveness and desperation in all of us. Rampant crime resulted in the decay of the area. Trash littered streets along with the sound of breaking bottles was the norm. I learned to embrace the sound of heavy traffic passing on School Street, gun threats, and the voices of passersby well into the night. Ironically, these sounds helped me to fall asleep.

During this time, I still had not realized that the things going on around me shouldn't be happening. I knew there were safer areas to be, but everyone experienced these situations, right? It's not that I was blind to the world. What I should have known was that these calamities made us different than everywhere else. Perhaps my parents kept me sheltered because they wanted me to be safe. All the gunshots, broken beer bottles, and gang fights in the world didn't come close to opening my eyes to how well I actually had it in this place some called the "ghetto." I considered myself equal among the rest, with all of us having the same issues with no degree of separation. All of us were poor, monetarily speaking, and we all shared the same experiences. I remember feeling low, that maybe the rest of the world didn't care about the hurt that accompanies poverty. Sometimes I still think this true.

One summer night I was playing basketball, a habit of mine for most summers when I was that young. Sometimes kids would randomly come from all over the neighborhood: kids from Fairview, Blaisdell, and even some who made their way from Talcott Page Park, which sat a few hills behind my home. A lot of times I would get compliments of being so good at playing basketball for a "white boy." This neighborhood was majority African American, so the sight of a scrawny white kid that could play basketball wasn't very common. Most of my friends growing up played basketball. Most of them were black, which increased my passion for the game. Because on the court, color was never an issue and neither was the world that we were living in at home. Everything went away once the ball was in your hand. You were equal to the next player and during those minutes you spent playing you felt as if nothing else in your life mattered. One opponent in particular never left my psyche, and even 15 years later I still can't help but wonder what became of him after we had finished our only game.

He had appeared from somewhere in the whereabouts of Avon Street through an unlit alleyway that ran from a dense and littered wooded area onto School Street. He watched me shoot around by myself and wanted to know if I'd like to play a quick game of one on one. Always up to a challenge, I immediately accepted. He seemed about the same age as me, same height and body build. We were both pretty scrawny and I thought this would be an easy win for me considering it was my "home court." It was getting dark and our only light was one that flickered on and off every few minutes above the hoop, but during these first few minutes I had noticed something astonishing that I failed to recognize when meeting him. I did not mention this to him because I didn't know how he would respond, but there was no way this was accidental, and I had been taught never to pry into someone's business.

So we continued playing with all of our emotions focused on our game. I remember him being fast, *really* fast. Although I was quick in my own respect, this kid was supremely gifted. He could get around me like I had never played the game of basketball and he seemingly shot with the best of them. I managed to keep the score close, but by the end of the game he had won. Darkness was upon us, and we shook hands. My expressionless face barely voiced an audible, but respectful, "good game." He disappeared back around Avon Street and that was the last I ever saw of him. I never got his name or found out where he lived. I never got to play with him again. Today, I couldn't even tell you what he looked like.

It wasn't my inability to have played with all the heart that I had. I *tried* to beat him. I used all my tricks, spins, dribbles, and hot spots on the court. He beat me fair and square on my own court with ease. I can't blame the diminishing light for my failure to win the game, as we both were disadvantaged by darkness. You learn a lot about yourself during a game of basketball. You learn what your limits are and how far you can push yourself. You learn a lot about your opponent as well; not just how they play the game of basketball, but their character during the game shows you their true personality outside of the game. He wasn't a rough player. There were no fouls in street ball and even if there were, we showed our toughness by not calling them on each other. To me this showed that he was competitive in nature and willing to sacrifice a little blood for the sense of accomplishment that comes with a big win. I had no excuse for losing. But it was this one pivotal game in my life that changed the entire perception I had of myself.

This kid, much like me who had been growing up in a slum neighborhood forgotten by the "enlightened," beat me in a basketball game *without shoes*. He had taken me to the hoop, used moves so fast even I couldn't keep up. And he did all of this without the most basic of necessities. This kid had notably experienced poverty in a much more extreme degree than I could ever imagine and used his personality on the court to show me that he was still equal to me by competing and beating me on a rocky court without a pair of shoes. He was barefoot, and I couldn't bring myself to ask him *why* this was. I just played the game the same way I had always played it. As I watched him run away back to where he came from, the only thing I can recall is his bare feet running over the gravel. Running over the broken glass and empty wrappers that comes with poverty-stricken neighborhoods. Running over all the beliefs that I once had of myself and my own well-being.

After that moment, I feared that I had made a big mistake. I used to be angry that my parents could not afford brand name shoes. My first pair of Air Jordans was a hand-me-down from my older brother when I was thirteen. No matter how worn and torn, I still had a pair of shoes to play basketball with. My parents always took care of my basic necessities. My perception of life after that game was changed forever. I no longer had the ambition to acquire things I did not need. I always told myself from that day on that there were people out there, *children* that would always need things they could not have. There would be no point for me to have emotional attachments to things I didn't need when there were children out there without basic necessities.

Over the next fifteen years of my life, I would frequently reflect on this moment. It inspired me to try and bring change to someone's life, *anyone's* life. It was a feeling of desperation that encompassed every emotion ever felt during the early years of my life living on School Street. I had made it out and went to school, received a college degree, and am now working a successful career. But what about the rest of the children back home? My heart didn't come with me when I left the "hood," it stayed right where it belonged. It stayed in that place where pain was rampant. It didn't follow me into white suburbia where rich kids feed off their parents' success. It stayed at that exact spot where a barefoot boy once beat me in a fair basketball game on a gravel court. I felt like I belonged with those kids because that was the place where I first experienced love, sorrow, and disaster. I didn't ask to be born in the ghetto of Rockford, Illinois, but I was, and for that I am thankful.

I still have yet to figure out how I can change those lives. The kids I grew up with are now grown. Some are in jail, some made it to college, some have kids of their own, and others are no longer with us. Growing up in these Rockford slums taught me that in order for one to succeed there are certain needs that must be met in order for them to pursue true actualization. My parents provided me my basic necessities. I knew I was still less fortunate than a lot of the world, but my fortune was supreme compared to barefoot children running through rocks, glass, and snake-ridden grass. If my hometown, as a collective people, does not provide the most basic of necessities for those in poverty, we will never make it out of our current state. Make all the tourist claims you want, but in the heart of the city there will always be pain and suffering hidden behind the curtains of green gardens and witty restaurant promotions.

The whereabouts of my opponent from that night will forever be unknown to me. His face has been forgotten by me and probably never known by those who could have helped him. Maybe he made it out of the ghetto and went to school, providing for himself and his family a better life that wasn't provided for him as a child. Or maybe his life succumbed to the pressures that so often take the lives of our children in an unintended direction. If I could go back, I would have asked for his name, learned about his life, and even perhaps have given him a pair of shoes to beat me again.

BETWEEN A TIF AND A HARD PLACE

ROCKFORD'S TAX INCREMENT FINANCING DILEMMA

TED BIONDO

Most cities have blighted areas in need of urban renewal. The challenge is how to attract private investors to these areas and to improve them by creating new growth and economic development. This investment would increase the overall value of the area and eventually provide more tax revenue for the city to fuel further growth and development. Ideally, the increased revenue would eventually become available to all area taxing districts and ultimately reduce or maintain taxes for existing taxpayers.

In 1977, the Illinois General Assembly passed the Tax Increment Allocation Redevelopment Act (65 ILCS 11-74.4-1). The Act authorized Illinois Municipalities to designate eligible areas for a period of 23 years that can then be developed or redeveloped through a Tax Increment Financing (TIF) district.

Initially in Rockford, TIF expenditures were often debt financed in anticipation of future tax revenues to pay off a bond or initial loans. TIF became increasingly popular in the 1980s and 1990s, when there were declines in subsidies for local economic development from federal grants, state grants, and federal tax subsidies.

It was to be a win-win for all concerned. The blighted area is improved, money is raised without having to raise taxes for economic development, and the (loss) of taxes during the 23 year period of the TIF isn't really a loss because, theoretically, the area was blighted and taxes would not have been increased in the area without the TIF.

TIF requires local taxing bodies to make a joint investment in the development or redevelopment of an identified, underperforming area, because those districts will obtain a return on their investment both when the TIF ceases and during future tax cycles.

After new development occurs in the blighted area, the assessed value of those improved properties will increase above the initial base Equalized Assessed Value (EAV) that existed when the TIF was created. This is called the Tax Increment EAV.

The Tax Increment EAV amount is then multiplied by the current tax rate of each taxing district and the County Clerk removes the TIF tax increment from each district prior to distributing the remaining taxes to those districts. This money is then deposited into the city Tax Increment Allocation Fund to make future investments in the TIF project areas and/or to repay any investment capital obtained by debt financing or bonds.

Investigation of last year's Winnebago County property tax bill, including pensions, shows the percentages of the total taxes that were paid by taxpayers to these municipalities: Rockford Schools (51.8%), Rockford City (21.8%), Winnebago County (7.3%), Parks (7.4%), Rock Valley College (3.5%), Rockford Library (3.4%) and 4.8% to other taxing bodies, including the airport, townships, and Forest Preserve.

Any reinvestment theoretically generates additional growth in property values within the TIF district, which results in even more revenue growth for reinvestment. In 23 years, taxpayers should see relief from these TIF areas to offset increases or future increases in taxes, in support the various taxing districts.

At least that's how it's supposed to work.

How do TIFs actually work in real life?

First, the TIF process works best for a truly "blighted" area. Also, property values should at least be generally increasing in other areas of the municipality or the Tax Increment EAV and its associated Tax increment will not increase for future development.

TIF is not a good economic development tool if property values are dropping. This year, the City of Rockford's total Tax Increment EAV has decreased to $30,809,162 from over $41.5M a couple of years ago, primarily due to decreasing property values.

At current tax rates, Rockford School District (RSD) 205 has $2,060,640 diverted to the Rockford Tax Increment Allocation Fund, the city itself pays $776,114, the county pays $290,314, the Park District pays $292,687, etc. The total paid is $30,809,162/100, multiplied by the current tax rate of 12.9016 = \$3,974,875 to Rockford. The city's Tax Increment was over \$5.4M in 2011.

If a TIF is set up in an area that is not blighted, an area that would have increased in value over time, with or without the TIF, then the other taxing districts are simply giving up tax revenue for 23 years to city coffers.

The other taxing districts do not have a final vote on the TIF districts; neither do the residents, who wind up in many cases supporting the TIFs through the city's General Fund for decades. City aldermen have the final vote on their municipal TIFs.

How is "blight" determined for a TIF District?

The decision that determines if an area is "blighted" rests entirely with a Joint Review Board (JRB) made up of various taxing district representatives as prescribed by state law. These are appointed members, not elected by the people, who determine by a majority vote, "if not but for the TIF," economic development would not have occurred.

If the JRB says the area is blighted, than a simple majority of the city aldermen is all that is required to approve a TIF. If the JRB determines the area is not blighted, then a 60% majority of the aldermen is required for approval.

A 60% vote of our aldermen should be the minimum requirement to approve a TIF that will remove any increase in assessed value from the tax rolls for a minimum of 23 years, regardless of the JRB vote.

Rockford Miracle Mile II TIF and the JRB's lack of concern

An example of the possible dysfunction of the JRB was exhibited in one recently proposed TIF district process, where the other taxing bodies simply failed to show up, even though tax revenue on a proposed Miracle Mile II TIF would be frozen for those districts for a minimum of 23 years.

The Rockford School District, Winnebago County, the Park District, Rock Valley College and all other taxing districts, representing almost 78% of our property tax bill, were no-shows for this important meeting.

The JRB meeting may not have even met the minimum requirements of the Open Meetings Act, which requires a quorum to be present to enact any business of a "Public Body" as the defined in 5 ILCS 120/Section 1.02 of the Act, such as dealing with decisions affecting public monies.

The city cast the lone vote to recommend that their municipal TIF move forward, rendering the entire JRB process suspect. Substitutes for the regular members of the taxing bodies should have been appointed to attend the JRB meeting.

I was not aware of any elected trustees at Rock Valley College or any members of the Winnebago County Board (I served on both at the time) that were informed of these JRB meetings, even though TIF approval affects property tax revenues of those taxing districts.

Therefore, unelected representatives in the taxing districts are making decisions on taxing policy for the elected officials, and not informing those officials of the meetings to get their input as representatives of the taxpayers. That was changed on those two boards!

The budgets reviewed by the Finance Committees of the taxing districts do not even include the tax revenue diverted to the city's TIFs, because it is removed prior to the taxing districts even receiving the money, thus bypassing transparency of tax dollars!

Why would the other taxing districts not attend the JRB Hearing?

Why would these other taxing districts not attend the meeting and simply let the city use this TIF area's tax increment increase for more than two decades without even one question being asked?

It's because the other taxing districts, with the exception of Rock Valley College, which is not subject to tax caps, simply raise their tax rates to meet their previous revenue plus inflation without voter approval under tax caps. The taxing districts have become complacent.

RVC can simply raise their tuition to achieve the same results.

Was the Proposed Miracle Mile II TIF District truly "Blighted?"

The proposed "blighted" TIF, which was to be discussed by the JRB, covered the area along East State Street bounded primarily by Alpine on the East and Mulford on the West, properties on both sides of East State on the south and extending roughly along the northern borders of the OSF Saint Anthony Medical Center Campus and the Rockford College Campus on the North, all within the city.

The TIF district actually begins just east of Mulford and includes Chase Bank and Rasmussen College, and the Shogun restaurant, across from one of the busiest malls in town, Forest Plaza and their associated businesses.

Since the city's economic development tool—the Tax Increment Finance district—is for blighted areas, I drove west on State Street from Mulford to Alpine to check the blight, pulling into parking lots, writing down the names of businesses in the proposed TIF area to observe if economic development was occurring in this area without TIF funding.

I then ventured to the Marketplace of Rockford Shopping Center, just west of Mulford on the north side of East State Street and discovered the newly opened Valli Produce, Oscars Pub, Old Time Pottery, Mobile, Culvers, and Walgreens.

On the south side of East State Street is Big K-Mart, Kentucky Fried Chicken, Long John Silvers, Dos Reales, Red Lobster, Lino's, Anderson and the Bachrodt's auto dealers, Northwest bank and Enterprise Rental with Furniture Row, Denver

Mattress, two antique Malls, Advanced Auto Parts, and Newton Plaza.

Crossing back on the North side of East State is OSF Hospital, Rockford Gastroenterology Center, Rockford Orthopedic, Rockford Cardiology, the Surgical Medical Building, OSF Specialty Clinic, OSF Medical Group, Davita Dialysis Nephrology Associates, and the OSF Center for Health, and a Pain Center—all included in the TIF area.

Further West on East State Street is Office Depot, Auto Glass, Aldi's Grocery, Panino's, Road Ranger, Versailles Place, Sherwin Williams Paint and of course, Rockford College with associated businesses, the YWCA, Primary Eye Care, College Center Office Park, Travel Inn, Sweden House, Manhattan Plaza, Forest City Motors, Happy Wok, Luigi's Pizza, a McDonald's, Ethan Allen, PNC Bank, Goodwill, and CVS drugs.

If East State Street between Alpine and Mulford is a "blighted" area, then all of Rockford must be blighted. Sure, there are some buildings in need of repair and overdue maintenance on parking lots with weeds growing through the cracks, but that's due to the recession, not blight.

University of Illinois Study on TIFs

The results of a study released in 2000 by the Institute and Public Affairs at the University of Illinois, based on an analysis of 235 municipalities in the metropolitan Chicago region, found cities, towns and villages that had TIF districts actually grew slower than those municipalities that did not have TIF districts.

The report also cited that some critics of TIFs simply say the municipalities use TIF to gain a greater portion of the property tax revenue at the expense of the other taxing districts in the municipality.

Another interesting observation of the study was, "If a TIF district simply redistributes growth from one part of the municipality to another, perhaps less suitable area, a municipality should grow at about the same rate or even more slowly overall than it would have otherwise."

Economic development dollars applied to more productive areas in Rockford, such as the Miracle Mile, and the Global trade sites, or East-side and South-side areas located by major transportation routes, may have increased the tax increment, raised more taxes for future growth. However, there are many reasons why certain areas of a municipality become "blighted" and TIF districts may not alter those reasons!

The study found that after accounting for many variables which might have affected growth, the 81 TIF municipalities' growth stayed about the same before and after a TIF was adopted, and the 154 municipalities without TIF grew faster than those who used it.

An additional finding was that within a TIF municipality, even non-TIF areas had less growth than a municipality that did not have a TIF district. TIF subsidies might help the growth within the TIF district, but hurts growth outside the TIF district by an even larger amount.

This is most likely because the other taxing bodies not receiving TIF funds still need revenue to cover their operating expenses over the 23 year period of the TIF, expenses that are increasing due to inflation and union contracts, but are not receiving revenue from the TIF districts.

When these other taxing districts extend their tax levies to provide services that may result from the growth itself, it sometimes results in higher property taxes outside the TIF districts, than would have been otherwise extended, especially if the TIF area is not actually blighted.

The study concluded that many businesses, even though being lured by the promise of cash incentives to move to a less desirable, "blighted" location, ultimately relocate to a better site in a different municipality, where it is more desirable to do business, and hence a more profitable location in the long run, even without the TIF incentives.

Since the total value of all taxable property in each taxing district determines the property tax rate needed to meet all revenue extensions—as property is removed from the tax rolls, the taxes on the remaining properties may increase.

Bottom line—the remaining taxpayers make up for any reduction in commercial or private property values being removed from the tax rolls, and that is compounded if a commercial property no longer exists to pay their corporate taxes.

The Effect of TIF on Taxes and Property values

In order for the TIF process to be a good deal for existing taxpayers, any cash balance left after the TIF expires should be distributed to all taxing districts and any increased assessed value of the TIF property needs to be returned to the tax rolls to provide relief for the taxpayers. The taxpayers are investors in this process. The city simply invests our money and there should be a return to the taxpayers.

The TIF Redevelopment Act allows the TIF districts' repayment time to be extended by 12 additional years for a total of 35 years! The state law also allows a tax increment to be transferred from a successful TIF district to an adjacent TIF district and to another TIF adjacent to the second TIF district—a process that has occurred in Rockford more than once.

So, what incentive is there for a new developer to invest in a business in a successful TIF, given that its tax increment balance may be taken and given to other projects outside the TIF district, rather than improve the district that produced the balance?

If a TIF has a balance at the end of the 23 years, the city may also establish a new TIF with the same boundaries and transfer the TIF balance to the "new" TIF rather than allowing the existing TIF area to expire, averting distribution of the tax increment balance to the other taxing bodies or placing the enhanced property on the tax rolls.

35 years is a long time to wait for any "new" economic development to contribute to the services that their growth may have imposed on the schools, libraries, parks, and the city, and county taxpayers.

After 35 years, some areas could actually depreciate in value and be deemed blighted again. What about the East-side, West-side and 7th Street TIF districts which are on their second 23 years, being reestablished on their original boundaries?

The City of Rockford is considering its 33rd TIF District having created a consolidated deficit for all existing TIF districts of $2.75M at the end of 2013, increasing to a deficit of $4.1M by 2022 - paid for the next decade from the city's operating funds, resulting in either higher property taxes or diverting funds from some other needed services.

So, adjacent successful TIF districts or the city's General Fund must pay the existing debt service for the consolidated TIF districts until there is a consolidated TIF balance. Based on current projections, Rockford's consolidated TIF districts won't have a positive balance until 2031, 18 years from now, and only two years before the TIFs expire, and that assumes that no new commitments are made in the interim.

The Role of Inflation in TIF usually not considered

Normal inflation may also cause property values within the TIF to appreciate, increases in value, which have nothing to do with the economic development that occurred due to the TIF, so the other taxing bodies lose that incremental EAV increase too.

There is also inflation in the costs of services provided by the other taxing districts that forego taxes for 23 to 35 years, compounded by any demand in growth of service due to TIF growth. With just 3% inflation, services after 24 years would double in cost.

Tax Increment Financing needs changes in the law.

Tax Increment Financing uses public funds to fund private development and taxpayers are on the hook if the TIF doesn't pan out, since the city obtains its funding from us, one way or another.

Some recommendations made by experts around the state call for reducing the number of years of tax benefit for TIF or at least allow the other taxing bodies to share the TIF tax increment in at least five year intervals, especially in contested areas of blight, where economic development might have been established in the area with or without the TIF during an economic recovery.

Limit the percentage of tax increment EAV in project area and total EAV within a municipality, otherwise you get the Chicago scenario, which has one-third of the city in TIF districts, with even in some of the most lucrative properties in downtown Chicago listed as "blighted." Miracle Mile II may be the beginning of Rockford's non-blighted TIF.

Greater Transparency Needed

TIF districts need to allow the economic development to apply to all taxing bodies and be transparent to all, so that taxpayers, who ultimately foot the bill in some way for these developments, receive some of the benefits in property tax relief.

TIF should also need to be on-budget, so property owners know how the successful TIF's money is being spent and where—on developments within the TIF or transferred to adjacent unsuccessful TIFs, which has been done in Rockford.

The TIF balances and/or deficits are there for all to see. However, the expenditures, the transfers between adjacent TIFs, the reasons for the transfers are all off budget.

The city council should have that data available to them by request. If for any reason that data is not provided, then the council member requesting the data should file a Freedom of Information Act (FOIA) request to obtain the information, as other elected officials have had to do recently in other taxing districts.

It's public information and should be made available to our elected representatives. The information is needed to understand the inner workings of the TIF process and to understand why the tool for economic development is not providing sufficient tax increment to repay the city's investments (maybe it's being used to pay debts).

All future TIFs should be pay as you go, because the taxpayers are getting tired of subsidizing $2M to $4M in loans that are floated through the General Fund or transferred from TIFs that work to TIFs that don't.

Joint Review Board process should be changed

The JRB should be under the Open Meetings Act. The duly elected boards from the other taxing districts should instruct their JRB representative of the elected board's decision on how to vote on the "blight" of a new TIF.

The state mandated meeting of the JRB should determine a percentage of any tax increment, which would be shared between the city and the other taxing bodies after intervals of five years, as the taxing districts did in the Rockton TIF with Chemtool.

The amount shared would be based on a formula that takes into account inflation and appreciation of the property, in addition to the tax increment increase over the 23 year period.

After that percentage is determined, the tax levy extensions of each taxing district would then be reduced by a smaller amount based on the levy paid to that TIF from each taxing district on a pro-rated basis.

That way, the economic development helps pay for all services provided by the other taxing bodies over the 23 year period of the TIF, and will reduce the pressure for each district to continually raise their taxes to the maximum allowed by the PTELL law.

Are Rockford TIFs bringing about economic development?

To answer the question are Rockford TIF districts working, we must ask "how many of the Rockford TIF districts have expired with a positive cash balance and placed a higher asset back on the tax rolls, than the blighted area that was there 23 or 35 years ago?" Did the positive cash balance go to the taxing districts, or was it rolled into another TIF?

TIF in this economy of decreasing home value, decreasing tax increment EAV, and decreasing tax increment have not provided the economic development goals for which they were intended. The TIF has been more of a drag on Rockford's economy than an asset for economic growth.

OF TRAGEDY AND TRIUMPH

THE BATTLE OVER ROCKFORD'S ABORTION CLINIC

KEVIN RILOTT

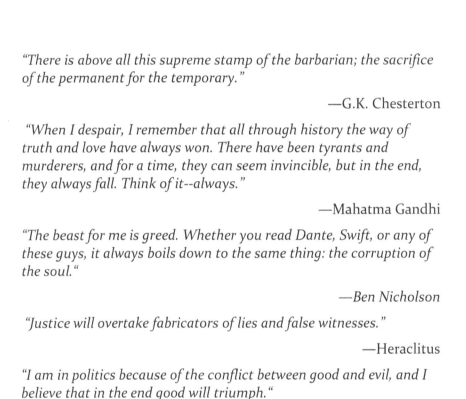

"There is above all this supreme stamp of the barbarian; the sacrifice of the permanent for the temporary."

—G.K. Chesterton

"When I despair, I remember that all through history the way of truth and love have always won. There have been tyrants and murderers, and for a time, they can seem invincible, but in the end, they always fall. Think of it--always."

—Mahatma Gandhi

"The beast for me is greed. Whether you read Dante, Swift, or any of these guys, it always boils down to the same thing: the corruption of the soul."

—Ben Nicholson

"Justice will overtake fabricators of lies and false witnesses."

—Heraclitus

"I am in politics because of the conflict between good and evil, and I believe that in the end good will triumph."

—Margaret Thatcher

"The abortion license has not brought freedom and security to women. Rather, it has ushered in a new era of irresponsibility toward women and children, one that now begins before birth."

—Gov. Robert Casey

This is the untold story of a terrible tragedy that took place in Rockford and the small group of heroic citizens who withstood threats, intimidation, and vile bigotry to save human lives and end the killing of unborn children in this city.

In 1973, Richard Ragsdale was waiting anxiously for a decision to be delivered by the United States Supreme Court concerning a case of an unidentified woman called Jane Roe against a Texas district Attorney named Henry Wade.

When *Roe v. Wade* was finally decided, Rockford physician Richard Ragsdale knew he had struck gold. Dr. Ragsdale was a man who was not squeamish about ending the life of a person in the womb, and this Supreme Court decision, along with its companion case *Doe v. Bolten*, just legalized abortion for all nine months of pregnancy.

Ragsdale immediately opened the doors to his new abortion clinic, the Northern Illinois Women's Center. This "clinic" was located inside Rockford Memorial Hospital and immediately attracted small but persistent protests.

From 1973-1985, Dr. Ragsdale preformed an untold number of abortions at that facility. Many people in Rockford (with the notable exception of a small group of Christians) paid little or no attention to what was happening behind the walls of what was considered a respected hospital.

Then everything changed. The public began to see ultrasound images of children in the womb. These clear and irrefutable pictures of little girls or boys sucking their thumb, yawning, opening and closing their beautiful hands, and even what looked like playing in the womb began to strike the conscience of the general public.

Then malpractice cases against Dr. Ragsdale began to mount. According to court documents, Ragsdale left parts of a baby inside more than one mother. Another mother was left with months of pain because of a botched abortion. Other documented court cases revealed that abortion, at least in Dr. Ragsdales case, could be very, very, dangerous.

Rockford Memorial Hospital had enough and Dr. Ragsdale and his abortion business was sent packing. That was when Ragsdale met a used car salesman name Gerald "Wayne" Webster. Webster had bought an old dilapidated school building at the corner of 10th and Broadway. In 1985, the Northern Illinois Women's Center set-up shop in the top floor of this building and Webster became its security guard.

This is when the Rockford pro-life community began a coordinated effort to offer love and support to any mother who was considering an abortion. In the beginning, large protests were held outside the abortion clinic attended by hundreds of pro-lifers and dozens of police officers. Occasionally, a few abortion supporters would show-up to counter protest.

Two "rescues" were held. Dozens of pro-lifers would file into the clinic on a day it was scheduled to perform abortions and sit in stairwells and hallways peacefully blocking access to the clinic. These protesters were arrested and hauled away. The police would have to carry the protesters out by their hands and feet and put them on a city bus that would take them to jail, but at least on those days, access to the clinic was blocked and no abortions took place. We have people alive today in the City of Rockford because of these actions.

While all this was taking place, a network of people who had a deep love for mothers and children was praying outside the Northern Illinois Women's Center every minute and every hour it was open for business.

Every day NIWC had abortions scheduled, sidewalk counselors were at the driveway offering help to any mother in need. Rockford pro-lifers helped mothers find jobs and a place to live, as well as maternity doctors. Mothers were helped with material needs as well as offered friendship and spiritual help. Thanks to these efforts, hundreds of children were saved from abortion.

When the clinic security guard saw that lives were being saved and the abortion clinic was losing money every time a mother chose life, he developed a plan that had the intention of driving pro-lifers away. In reality, it only exposed the philosophy and true nature of "choice" in Rockford.

While Christians were silently praying on the sidewalks outside of NIWC, clinic security guard Webster would get on his loud public address system and play sexually explicit recordings filled with pornographic and blasphemous attacks on God, women, and children. The intention was to drive away from the clinic the people who were praying for and offering help to mothers considering abortion.

When this failed, Webster turned it up a notch. He began posting the names, addresses, and phone numbers of pro-lifers in the windows of the clinic with the intention of intimidating them into not returning. When this failed as well, Webster would get on his loud speakers and call out the addresses of individual pro-lifers and asked, "Who is watching your house while you are here?"

A spiritual battle was developing between a group of people who wanted to offer love and support to mothers and children and those inside the clinic who were becoming very rich off ending human lives in the womb.

Webster and Ragsdale tried all they could to block mothers from receiving aid and information about alternatives to abortion. Webster would appear in the driveway of the clinic dressed as a Priest. He would motion to cars carrying mothers to not to stop and talk with the sidewalk counselors, but drive into the clinic parking-lot. When this failed, Webster dressed as the devil and rented a sewage truck that he threatened to spray pro-lifers with. He even had someone dress up as Cookie Monster from Sesame Street to distribute condoms to neighborhood children. He hoped, I believe, to drum up business for his abortion clinic when these young people became sexually active and their contraception failed.

Visitors to the Northern Illinois Women's Center told pro-lifers and public health officials about the bad smells and ugly conditions inside the clinic. Even from the outside, moldy walls and rotted ceilings that were caving in could be seen through the upper floor windows.

Because of these conditions, and the general disregard for women's health found in the abortion industry, in 1989 Dr. Ragsdale filed a lawsuit, *Ragsdale v. Turnock,* in the State of Illinois that sought the removal of almost all medical standards for abortion clinics. This included laboratory tests, post-operative care, preparation for emergencies, abortion counseling, and believe it or not even the requirement that a woman must have a positive pregnancy test before undergoing an abortion.

In a backroom deal with pro-abortion politicians, abortionist Ragsdale got what he wanted; nearly the complete removal of medical standards for abortion clinics. This case has had profound national effects, and since then we have seen countless abortion mills around the country treating women in conditions that would not pass inspection for an animal kennel.

Then, in 1994, the philosophy of "choice" reared its ugly face again as Rockford abortionist Richard Ragsdale and his wife were indicted on four counts of child pornography involving their three-year-old foster daughter.

One of the photographs reportedly showed the child dressed in black lace thong panties, with her genitalia and buttocks exposed. It had been the technician at the lab who had seen the photos and was so disturbed by them he contacted the police.[1] Ragsdale was charged with possession of the photographs, which he picked up after they were developed. Ragsdale told reporters that the situation was a "minor family matter."

The charges against both Ragsdale and his wife were dropped after his wife signed a "statement of fact" admitting that the photographs "were of an inappropriate nature and could constitute a violation of state law."[2] The child was placed in another

---

[1] "Abortion Doctor Faces Porn Charge," *Chicago Tribune* (Chicago) 24 September 1994.

[2] "Child Porn Charges Are Dropped," *Chicago Tribune* (Chicago) 17 November 1994.

foster home by child protective services upon the Ragsdales' arrest, and was later adopted by an out-of-state family.

As the years passed, Christians continued to stand outside the clinic on below zero mornings in January, through rainy days in April, and sweltering hot days in July. Thousands of lives were ended in the soiled conditions of the abortion clinic, but hundreds of mothers chose life with the help of these good Christian people. Some stood at the driveway of the clinic offing help, while others stood on the sidewalks outside the abortion mill and offered thousands upon thousands of hours of prayer for the lives of the unborn.

Two people who must always be remembered when the history of the Rockford abortion clinic is discussed are Don and Mary Brady of the Rockford *Labor News*. The *Labor News* was a union newspaper for decades in Rockford. In Fact, it was Cap Brady, Don's Father and founder of the *Labor News*, who ran an illegal abortionist named Dr. Shipley out of Rockford in the 1950s.

The *Labor News* building was located next to the abortion clinic on Broadway. Don and Mary offered a refuge to pro-lifers for nearly 30 years. Any person who needed a break from sidewalk counseling or praying on the sidewalks could go to the *Labor News* building for a cup of coffee, a donut, or a warm smile and words of encouragement from the Bradys. For three decades, the *Labor News* ran stories of lives saved from abortion and the struggle to respect and protect all human life. The Brady family was threatened and at times lost business because of their defense of life, but they never wavered. Many mothers had the chance to speak to pro-lifers in the quiet of the *Labor News* office, and it was in this building they decided to choose life.

On October 23, 2004, after spending over 20 years stopping the beating hearts of children in the womb, Richard Ragsdale died of cancer. Before he entered into eternity to receive the judgment of God, Ragsdale turned the Northern Illinois Women's Center over to fellow abortionist Dennis Christensen.

Christensen was the owner of an abortion clinic in Madison and another located near the border of Michigan and Indiana.

The Northern Illinois Women's Center had a long history of harming women, ending the lives of children, and bizarre and vicious attacks on the people of Rockford. Now, abortionist Christensen removed all restraints from his clinic security guard, Wayne Webster. The Northern Illinois Women's Center would become known not only in America but around the world as the most racist, bigoted, and depraved so-called medical facility in the United States.

In the late 1980s and into the 1990s, the Rockford abortion clinic had been ending the lives of approximately 50-75 babies a week. Through the constant efforts of committed Christians offering love and support to mothers in need, that number began to steadily decline to approximately 20-40 a week by the mid-1990s.

When Christensen took over NIWC, both he and Webster knew they needed to silence the sidewalk counselors and people who were constantly praying outside of the clinic if they wanted their abortion business to survive. Webster set in motion a plan of action that turned up the threats and intimidation against the pro-lifers to a level of viciousness not seen anywhere else in the country.

First we will look at some of the attempts of intimidation that took place by Wayne Webster, the clinic security guard.

"Wayne," as he was known by people in the Broadway neighborhood, began putting up a series of signs in the abortion clinic widows using profanity and attacking God that were aimed at demoralizing and intimidating the Christians outside into losing their zeal for protecting human life.[3]

What we have to remember is these signs, symbols, and actions were being directed and carried out by the staff of a medical facility in Rockford that had treated upwards of 100,000 people. These signs and actions were a clear indication of how patients were treated, what kind of care they received, and what the staff thought of mothers and children. If any other medical facility or

---

[3] Thaddeus M. Baklinski, "Rockford Abortion Mill Hits New Low In Grotesque Window Dressing," *Catholic Exchange*, http://catholicexchange.com/rockford-abortion-mill-hits-new-low-in-grotesque-window-dressing (1 June 2010).

business in the city of Rockford did these things, an outraged community would have closed them years ago.

These actions and signs that were place in the clinic doors and windows included:

- Placing a rubber chicken over the body of Jesus Christ on a Crucifix.
- Putting the names of pro-lifers husbands or wives on signs with intimidating messages.
- Placing a nun doll in coffin with "voodoo" pins in it.
- The clinic security guard walking around the parking-lot trying to intimidate people with a chainsaw.
- Numerous pictures desecrating the image of Jesus Christ.
- Placing a mask of a demon in the clinic window.
- Rubber chickens hanging by nooses. These nooses offended many African Americans (one time when an African America grandfather who was with his granddaughter at the clinic saw the nooses he immediately knew the racist symbolism they represented and convinced his granddaughter not to abort her baby).
- Numerous signs mocking people with the HIV virus, including a large sign in an entrance to the clinic declaring Christians have the HIV virus (no other medical facility or business in the county could ever get away with this kind of bigotry).
- A sign claiming God would not give a dog HIV but would give it to Christians.
- A sign claiming people with HIV would go to Hell.
- Crucifixes hanging by nooses with wording on them mocking God.
- Signs claiming the deceased relative of pro-lifers are in Hell.
- A picture of Jesus giving the finger with the words, "Even Jesus hates you." This sign was placed by the door that women used when they left the clinic after an abortion. The devastating effect of this sign on a post-abortive mother could not be exaggerated.

- A sign celebrating the 50,000th abortion performed by the Rockford abortion clinic that included words mocking Jesus, claiming He was only able to save 50 babies from abortion.
- A sign calling a pro-lifer's wife a "whore" and listing the sexual acts the clinic said she performed. The sign also gave her address and phone number.

Webster then began working closely with a man named Keith who would stand at the abortion clinic driveway and call pro-lifers "niggers" (no matter if they were black or white), sometimes using the "n-word" dozens of times in just a few minutes. Keith would go on and on about how he loved the smell of burning baby bodies that he claimed came from the clinic chimney.[4]

When Keith would threaten pro-lifers and the police were called, Webster would be sitting in the clinic listening to his police scanner and would warn Keith over the public address system when the police were about to arrive. Keith would then quickly leave the clinic and come back at a later time. According to eyewitnesses, on more than one occasion, he reportedly vandalized the cars of pro-lifers and would pull a knife out of his pocket in an attempt to intimidate them.

The clinic put up scores of other signs of hatred toward God, women, children, and Christians. We all know our world contains bigots, but to have these bigots running a medical facility in Rockford is another thing. These signs and symbols of pure depravity were an outward sign of what was taking place behind the walls of the Northern Illinois Women's Center.

The attacks by abortion clinic staff only strengthened the resolve of pro-lifers to protect mothers and children from what was taking place inside the clinic. Webster then enlisted the aid of Rockford's 11th Ward Alderman Karen Elyea. Elyea, who had been

---

[4] "Hate Crime Charge Filed over Verbal Assault against Pro-Lifers: "Ni**er! You are a worthless degener[ate]," LifeSiteNews.com, http://www.lifesitenews. com/news/archive//ldn/2009/apr/09040310 (3 April 2009).

charged, but not convicted, with selling drug paraphernalia and possessing and selling cannabis in 2003, made a good partner for Webster in his attempt block help for mothers in need.[5]

Elyea and Webster tried to convince the Rockford City Council to place a "bubble zone" around the clinic to prevent mothers from receiving help.[6] They failed miserably when the full City Council was shown the history of racism and bigotry directed towards the people of Rockford by the clinic staff.

The next thing Elyea did was recruit a young police officer to try and stop pro-lifers from holding signs on the sidewalk. The officer, who was new to the clinic beat, followed the alderman's orders and made a pro-lifer remove his sign. It only took a call to a police supervisor to end this pathetic attempt at stopping free speech. Officers were told not to follow her instructions where the clinic was concerned.

When a group of Rockford citizens contracted with TLC Pregnancy Services mobile ultrasound van to offer free ultrasounds to any mother in need outside of the clinic, Webster and Alderman Elyea pulled out all the stops to block mothers from seeing the truth that children in the womb are beautiful living human beings.

The clinic began to realize that mothers who were scheduled for abortions were choosing life instead because they had the opportunity see the baby in their womb in the ultrasound van.[7] Webster, the former used car dealer, parked dozens of used cars throughout the neighborhood around the clinic so the van would not have a place to park. When this effort failed because mothers were still using the ultrasound van even if it had to park blocks away, Webster and Elyea attempted to have the van blocked by city ordinance from parking anywhere in Rockford.

---

[5] People of the State of Illinois vs. Karen Lynn Elyea, Case #2003-CF-0000145 and 2003-CF-0000146 (15 January 2003).

[6] "Committee delays action on proposed abortion 'bubble' ordinance," *Rock River Times* (Rockford) 27 January–2 February 2010.

[7] Mark Pickup, "Ultrasound's image saves unborn lives," *Western Catholic Reporter,* http://www.wcr.ab.ca/Columns/OpinionsStories/tabid/70/entryid/1012/Default.aspx (11 May 2011).

In 2010, a fight erupted on the Rockford City Council between a group of aldermen who sided with Elyea and attempted to block the ultrasound van and a group of aldermen who supported it.

In the end, it was the courageous efforts of Rockford Mayor Lawrence J. Morrissey, who bypassed the City Council and granted the mobile ultrasound a special use permit to park in Rockford, that broke the stalemate. Mayor Morrissey granted the first special use permit on Good Friday, 2010. On this Good Friday, while 100 people were praying the Stations of the Cross outside the clinic, God answered their prayers and rewarded the faith of Mayor Morrissey when two mothers used the mobile ultrasound to choose life. This truly was a Good Friday.

Abortion proponents were extremely frustrated. James, Aldermen Elyea's former live-in boyfriend, showed up on the sidewalk of the clinic and began screaming at a pro-lifer who was offering help to a mother in need. When James saw another pro-lifer videotaping his tirade, he charged at the photographer and began licking the lens of the camera.[8] The police were called, but when they arrived, they looked as perplexed as everyone else. What do you do with a man who walks around the streets of Rockford licking camera lenses?

This clinic's disregard for public health and common decency would end up being its own undoing, and *Ragsdale v. Turnock* set the stage. Once you remove common sense safety regulations, even the minimal standards that are left seem to be of no importance. After a decade of pro-lifers pleading with the State of Illinois to inspect the Northern Illinois Women's Center, that inspection final took place in 2011.

The results below are taken directly from the Illinois Department of Public Health Report that shocked even veteran public health officials.

---

[8] Al, "Just When You Think Things Can't Get Any More Bizarre @ the Rockford Abortion Clinic," *Is Anybody There?*, http://al007italia.blogspot.com/2010/08/just-when-you-think-things-cant-get-any.html (6 August 2010).

- 3 of 3 operating rooms inspected failed to ensure a sanitary environment.
- NIWC failed to prevent potential contamination of clean equipment.
- The Autoclave that is used to sterilize surgical equipment failed biological inspection.
- Gynecological cannulas (surgical instruments inserted inside a woman's vagina) were stained with a "brown substance."
- Shoes were stored inside an open box of surgical gloves.
- Operating room #1 contained a box of opened surgical gloves stained with a dried brown substance.
- NIWC did not have a registered nurse in the operating room for over three years. It didn't even have one on its payroll. Unqualified and unlicensed personnel were doing the work of a professional nurse.

What these results showed was that the Northern Illinois Women's Center was an unsanitary and dangerous abortion mill that was a real threat to every mother who entered its doors. When an Illinois Public Health official was asked about the possibility of STDs being transmitted from one woman to another because the autoclave (a machine that is used to sanitize surgical instruments) was not working, the response was, "It's a very real possibility for any procedure that took place in the last year."

It is reasonable to ask how such a facility could be operating in the heart of Rockford for so long. One of the main reasons, I believe, was the failure of the Rockford *Register Star* to report the facts concerning this medical clinic that for decades made a very public display of the most vicious racism, bigotry, and discrimination Rockford has ever seen. We all know that if any other medical facility in Rockford promoted and used this kind of sickening hatred it would have been front page news.

When the news broke that NIWC failed its health inspection and was closed by the State, the *Register Star* refused to print any explanation of what the conditions were really like inside the abortion mill. The *Register Star* only reported that they were closed.

Through this failure of journalism, the Rockford *Register Star* let the women of Rockford place their lives in the hands of a medical facility that publicly promoted the most perverse and heinous public attacks in the history of Rockford. Then, when the dangerous and possibly life threatening conditions inside this abortion mill were discovered by the State of Illinois, the *Register Star* refused to print or explain the horrific details of this dangerous place.

That the *Register Star* has promoted abortion, even partial birth abortions, in its editorials is one thing.[9] To keep these facts from the women of Rockford, however, shows "choice" is not about women's health, but about maintaining at any cost the political power to end the lives of children in the womb.

Through all of this, sidewalk counselors stood at the driveway of the clinic every hour of every day to offer help to expectant mothers. People of all ages continued to pray and hold signs on the sidewalks outside.

Starting in 2009, a group of Catholic Priests began offering prayers of exorcism outside of the Rockford abortion clinic every week. A Protestant Minister walked up and down the sidewalks praying and offering encouragement to everyone he would meet. On one occasion, when a father arrived at the clinic in the hope of convincing his girlfriend not to have an abortion, it was a beautiful sight to see the Minister and Priest arm in arm leading Catholics and Protestants in prayer together. And yes, the young mother came out of the mill a short time later and chose life.

In September 2011, the Northern Illinois Women's Center was closed by the state of Illinois as a danger to public health. NIWC spent months attempting to reopen, but the level to which

---

9 "Our view: Abortion clinic's demise will limit women's choices," *Register Star* (Rockford) 14 January 2012; "This newspaper has supported a woman's right to choose for decades. We regret the loss of yet another abortion provider..."

they had sunk made it impossible for them to turn that place into a safe medical environment. In January 2012, NIWC announced they had given up their efforts to reopen and would close forever.

In a fitting epitaph to the closing of the most abhorrent, bigoted, and hate filled facility of any kind in America, Dr. Alveda King, the niece of the Rev. Martin Luther King, came to Rockford on January 26, 2012 to offer prayers of thanksgiving outside of the now closed abortion mill and to thank God for the lives that would now be saved.

You may have wondered why the names of Rockford pro-lifers were not used in this story. It is for two reasons. First, there were too many women, men, and young people over the 28 year history of the Rockford abortion mill who defended life, prayed, helped mothers in need, who outlasted the attacks of the abortion mill staff, and saved the lives of babies, to mention in this article.

The second reason is that none of these people ever gave of their time or love to receive recognition. They served mothers and children in need in order to make Christ present in our community, to let mothers who were considering abortion know they are loved, and to save children in the womb from death.

Seeing a mother's face who had just chosen life or holding in their arms a beautiful baby who had been saved from death was all the reward they ever hoped for.

From 1973 to 2012, a life and death struggle took place in Rockford between the culture of death and a people of life. An estimated 75,000 human lives were ended inside of the Northern Illinois Women's Center. This filthy, shameless, and dangerous killing center used every form of intimidation they could think of to keep mothers from choosing life.

In the end, life won.

A Long, Dark Night

The Simon Peter Nelson Murders

Michael Kleen

The man's heart raced as the inky black road passed under the headlights of his green station wagon. Sweat collected on his forehead, and he frequently removed his glasses, which were freckled with tiny dark stains, to clear it away. He could see the bright lights of Milwaukee in the distance.

Almost there.

The trip seemed unreal. Had he been driving an hour? Two? He did not know. The nightmare of home and the overwhelming drive to put an end to everything ruled his mind.

Finally, he was in the city. Everything seemed strangely quiet. The road was empty, and the parked cars he passed glistened with midnight frost. Suddenly the hotel sprang up in front of him. Rows and rows of vertical red brick between sets of windows on its exterior reminded him of the bars of a jail cell.

Inside Room 425, Ann let the beige, plastic handset fall back onto the phone receiver for the final time. She sat on the edge of the bed. Ernie looked worried and rested his hand on her shoulder. Suddenly, there was a knock at the door—a loud, ominous thud.

Ernie walked past a bouquet of wilting autumn flowers. A card reading, "Love, Peter" lay discarded on the edge of the dresser, precariously hovering over the wastepaper basket. He hesitantly opened the door and peered into the dimly lit hallway. A large, hulking man stood there. His face was flushed and his short hair wet and tussled.

It was Ann's husband.

"I just want to say goodbye," he stammered. "Just one kiss goodbye, please."

A flash of sympathy overcame Ann, and she motioned for him to come into the room.

"Call a priest," her husband said, nearly inaudibly. Strength returned to his voice. "I told you to call a priest. Call two priests and then call the police."

Ernie glanced at Ann. She nodded, and he headed out the door and down the hall to the lobby.

Scared and frustrated, Ann demanded, "Where are the kids?"

"They're dead!" her husband shouted. The words burst out with a flash of anger tinged with spite. "They are all dead! How do you feel about that?"

Prelude to Tragedy

January 1978 was, up to that year, the fifth coldest January on record in Rockford. Moviegoers huddled in their coats and packed the Midway Theater to see *Saturday Night Fever*, a film tribute to disco starring a young, up-and-coming actor named John Travolta. Earlier that winter, the Rockford area recorded the state's largest drop in unemployment, from 6.7 percent in mid-November to 4.6 percent in mid-December. This was largely due to the reopening of the Chrysler assembly plant in Belvidere.

On the ninth floor of the Talcott Building (321 W. State St.), Simon Peter Nelson, 46, was doing his part at Management Recruiters, Inc. to help fill local job openings. He was a large man, 6 foot 2 inches tall, weighing nearly 300 pounds, with thick glasses, unkempt hair, and a beard. His wife, Ann, 38, was a former medal-winning ice skater from Indianapolis, Indiana. She was thin, with short, wavy hair and a handsome face. The couple had met in February, 1964 and married about eight months later. "She was the most beautiful girl I'd ever seen," Nelson later testified in court.[1]

Five of Simon and Ann's six children, ranging in age from three to twelve, had returned to school from Christmas break on Tuesday, January 3rd. Jennifer, the oldest, had just transferred to St. Peter's School earlier that year. Simon, Jr., 10; Andrew, 8; Matthew, 7; and Rose Ann, 5, attended Walker Elementary School, which was located a few blocks from the Nelsons' home in Rockford's Churchill's Grove neighborhood. David, the youngest, was not yet attending school.

---

[1] "Nelson tells of troubled life," *Register-Star* (Rockford) 20 May 1978.

The Nelson family moved to Rockford in the spring of 1976, after spending several years living in Beloit, Wisconsin. Simon Peter Nelson, who preferred the name "Pete," owned a management consulting firm called Businessmen's Clearinghouse, Inc. in the Rockford Trust Building. He commuted to Rockford between 1971 and November 1975, when his business folded. Ann was working as an ice skating instructor in Janesville when the couple decided to move to Rockford. They purchased a Dutch Colonial home at 1425 Camp Avenue and lived off Ann's trust fund while Nelson bounced from job to job. Susan, Simon Peter Nelson's 20-year-old daughter from a previous marriage, lived with them until the fall of 1977.

While Nelson's friend, Michael Weldon, ultimately hired him as a job-placement interviewer for his company, Management Recruiters, Inc., Ann began working as an instructor at the Riverview Ice House in Rockford. Simon Peter Nelson was, by all accounts, likable and charming. According to Weldon, Nelson's business venture failed in part because he had a tendency to make friends with his clients, even inviting them over to his house for drinks. He took a personal interest in their progress, and called them even when he was off the clock. Despite this effort, he never made more than $14,000 a year (around $53,000 in 2013 dollars).[2]

According to their friends and neighbors, the Nelsons settled into a modest but happy life in Rockford. "They were quiet and fit right in with the neighborhood, but I think very few people knew them well," John Bates, a next door neighbor, told the Rockford *Register-Star*. Likewise, William Smardo, who lived on the opposite side of 1425 Camp Ave., knew Simon Peter Nelson had been having problems securing a job, but nothing more serious.[3] It was common knowledge that Nelson consumed alcohol on a near-nightly basis, but not to the point of severe intoxication. Judy Terasaki, whose daughter took ice skating lessons from Ann Nelson, described Ann as very patient and easy going. "I can't think of a time I ever saw her mad," she told the *Register Star*. "Ann was a

[2] "Things were routine, until the end," *Morning Star* (Rockford) 10 January 1978; *Register-Star* (Rockford) 20 May 1978.

[3] "Neighbors watch, shocked," *Register-Star* (Rockford) 7 January 1978.

good teacher and woman," Ann Kanter, whose daughter also took lessons at the Riverview Ice House, agreed. "She loved kids and she loved to skate." She added, "She was so good with the kids."[4]

There were, however, rumors of neglect. John and Sandy Bates, who lived at 1427 Camp Ave., told detectives that Simon and Ann went away for extended periods of time and left their eldest daughter, who was 12-years-old, to look after the rest of the children. When John and Sandy did see the Nelson children, "they always appeared to be dirty, and in many instances ill clothed, such as no shoes and socks in cold weather." The Bates children, who sometimes played with the Nelson children, told their parents that "On occasion, Simon Nelson would tie his children to a chair and then beat them."[5]

William and Cathleen Smardo, who lived at 1421 Camp Ave., agreed. Cathleen had babysat for the two youngest Nelson children, Rose Ann and David, from September 1976 to March 1977. Although they were not much more than infants at the time, the children would walk over to her home unescorted. "When it was cold it was not uncommon to see the Nelson children come over only wearing a diaper and an undershirt, also wearing boots but no shoes or socks underneath the boots," Cathleen told detectives. "The two children were always dirty and it appeared as though they were never bathed..." She also explained that Simon and Ann Nelson would leave for the day and place Jennifer, their oldest, in charge of the other children.[6]

Jennifer Nelson was well-liked. "She was very quiet," Kelly Snider, one of Jennifer's friends at St. Peter's School, told the *Register-Star*. "She never talked about any home problems at all."[7] Like her mother, Jennifer showed talent on the ice. She and a

---

[4] "Skating families gather to share sorrow," *Register-Star* (Rockford) 7 January 1978.

[5] M. Emigholz #106, *Supplementary Report, Case #943-263* (Rockford Police Dept., 7 January 1978), Records No. 270.

[6] Ibid., Records No. 271.

[7] "Disbelief haunts friends at slain children's home," *Register-Star* (Rockford) 8 January 1978.

partner had won the preliminary dance competition in the Wagon Wheel Open in the summer of 1977. Donald Swanson, Principal of Walker Elementary School, described her as "another Janet Lynn."[8] Janet Lynn Nowicki, who moved to Rockford at the age of eight, won the bronze medal in women's figure skating at the 1972 Winter Olympics.

Despite appearances to the contrary, all was not well in the Nelson home. The family was running out of money. Ann Nelson's trust fund had dwindled to almost nothing by the end of 1977, and the family was wallowing in debt. Simon Peter Nelson spent many hours after work at local taverns. His favorite bar was Mike and Dale's Lounge, formerly located in the Lafayette Hotel building at 202 N. Church Street. In addition to being Nelson's boss at Management Recruiters, Inc., Michael Weldon was co-owner of that establishment. He told detectives, "More often than not, in the evenings, when Ann would be skating, [Nelson] would leave the kids, with the 12-yr. old daughter totally in charge... It seemed that he would either leave work, go home, spend an hour or two on the phone work related, and then leave home. Or he wouldn't go home at all, but go straight to the lounge, often times closing it down."[9]

The couple began to argue more frequently, and Nelson claimed his wife "crudely berated him and criticized his sexuality." He testified in court that, "She seemed to be moving further away from me and the kids and the home and spent more time away. It seemed to be a rejection of all of us."[10] The couple talked about getting a divorce over the Christmas holiday, but Nelson asked Ann to take some time and think it over. She agreed.

A burgeoning relationship between Ann Nelson and one of her male students, Ernest (Ernie) Johnson, 30, seemed to accelerate the deterioration of Ann and Simon's marriage. Ernie and his wife Linda (Lynn) were friends of the Nelsons and had recently moved to suburban Milwaukee, Wisconsin, where Ernie took a job at

---

[8] "Skating career lost to death," *Register-Star* (Rockford) 8 January 1978.
[9] Kris Dickinson #82, *Statement of Michael Weldon, Case #943-263* (Rockford Police Dept., 7 January 1978), Records No. 315.
[10] *Register-Star* (Rockford) 20 May 1978.

Wilson Foods. The couple still made the trip to Rockford on weekends for ice skating lessons with Ann. According to Don Lumley, manager of the Riverview Ice House, and Carol Ueck, Lesson Coordinator, rumors about Ann and Ernie began sometime in the summer of 1977. After the Johnsons moved to the Milwaukee area, they came to Rockford on the weekends to skate socially with Ann at the Wagon Wheel, have dinner with the Nelson family, and then come to Riverview on Sunday for a lesson. Ann spoke with Ms. Ueck on the phone from time to time, and she told her that there was "nothing physical" between her and Ernie.[11] Later, she told investigators that Ernie's wife, Lynn, and she used to be friends, but when Ernie and Lynn began to have marital problems, Lynn "lashed out" at both Ann and Ernie's devotion to ice skating. As for Ernie, Ann said that sometimes skating served as an escape and that she was part of Ernie's "escape."[12]

On Tuesday, January 3rd, Ann told Ms. Ueck that Ernie Johnson was asking his wife for a divorce, that Lynn was hysterical, and that she was threatening to call the Park District Manager. Lynn had begun to suspect something was going on between her husband and Ann. Ms. Ueck shared those suspicions, and said that "certain things had become rather obvious" to everyone who worked at Riverview. She advised Ann to put some distance between herself and Ernie. The next night, Ann, Ernie, and Lynn were skating at the Riverview Ice House when Simon Peter Nelson came down to "diffuse the bomb" between Ernie and Lynn. He spoke with the Johnsons outside, then Nelson and Ernie went to the Cart (formerly located in the Lafayette Hotel building at 206 N. Church St.) while Lynn went to the Nelsons' home to cool off. Nelson later picked up Ann and brought her to the Cart sometime after 10:30pm.[13]

---

[11] Kris Dickinson #82 and R. Bast, *Supplementary Report, Case #943-263* (Rockford Police Dept., 9 January 1978), Records No. 442.

[12] Kris Dickinson #82, *Supplementary Report, Case #943-263* (Rockford Police Dept., 13 January 1978), Records No. 2341-2342.

[13] Dickinson and Bast, Records No. 442-443.

Like Lynn, Simon Peter Nelson was jealous of the time Ernie spent with Ann, but did not quite suspect an affair. He told detectives that he thought Ernie or another man who worked at the skating rink might have come between them, but that he was not sure because they were seeing each other for "professional reasons."[14] He also mentioned his feelings to psychologists who interviewed him after his arrest. His jealousy seemed to be directed at Ann's devotion to ice skating in general, as well as "all the married males that were [her] students."[15]

Nelson could sense there was substance to Ann's threats of divorce, and he made a desperate attempt to reform his self-image. After all, there was light on the horizon. According to Michael Weldon, Nelson was on track to make $30,000 to $40,000 in 1978, nearly three times his current income.[16] Nelson cut his hair, shaved his beard, and began a fitness program at the YMCA. More importantly, he quit drinking. Weldon noticed dramatic improvement in his work habits and his relationship with his kids. "He made a concerted effort to go out and get things for his kids for Christmas that they would really like," Weldon told detectives. "He didn't have a lot of money, and I gave him a small advance. He'd come back loaded down with packages, and seemed to enjoy getting things for the kids. He really was going all out for the kids, and it seemed different from how he'd been on other Christmases."[17] Around the second week of December, Nelson traded in his old Volkswagen for a four-door, green 1970 Pontiac Catalina Station Wagon. He believed it was a more appropriate vehicle for a family of their size.

According to Ann, sometime around Christmas her husband began reading the book *Anatomy of a Murder* (1958) by Robert Traver. In court, she testified that she had observed Nelson

---

[14] R. Donnelli #115 and Otwell, *Supplementary Report, Case #943-263* (Rockford Police Dept., 9 January 1978), Records No. 426.

[15] Carl H. Hamann, M.D., to Judge John S. Ghent, 16 May 1978. Winnebago County 17th Judicial Circuit Court, Case No. 78-CF-23.

[16] *Register-Star* (Rockford) 20 May 1978.

[17] Dickinson, *Statement of Michael Weldon,* Records No. 314.

reading the book shortly after Christmas, at which point he was about two-thirds of the way through. After New Year's Day, 1978, she again observed him reading *Anatomy of a Murder*, but that time he was about one-fourth of the way through the book, suggesting that Nelson had started reading it for a second time.[18] Written under a pseudonym by a former Michigan Supreme Court justice, *Anatomy of a Murder* dramatizes a trial in which the defendant is acquitted of murder by reason of insanity. It became a bestselling novel and was turned into a film starring Jimmy Stewart and George C. Scott.

On Thursday, January 5th, the morning after Ann, Simon, and Ernie Johnson discussed the Johnsons' pending divorce at a quiet bar in the Lafayette Hotel, Simon Peter Nelson drove his wife to the Downtown Ramada Inn (633 West Michigan Street) in Milwaukee, Wisconsin. He paid $60.00 cash for a two night stay. Nelson had suggested Ann stay with the Johnsons in Milwaukee over the weekend to work things out. Unbeknownst to Nelson, the couple's longtime friend and attorney, Karl Winkler, also urged Ann to get away for a few days to mull over her own thoughts of divorce.[19] She told friends, neighbors, and coworkers that she was visiting relatives in Indianapolis.

The Night Simon Fell to Pieces

Friday, January 6, 1978 was a day of celebration for many of Rockford's civic leaders. After years of planning and negotiation, the State of Illinois had finally approved the city's Metro Centre application. The state agreed to sell $15.3 million in bonds to help fund the project in the heart of downtown Rockford. The Rockford Metro Centre was to be a 213,000-square-foot public arena with a seating capacity of 10,078. "This is a tremendous day in the history of Rockford," Rockford Community Development Director Ed

---

[18] People v. Nelson, Appellate Court of Illinois, Second District, 92 Ill. App. 3d 35 (1980).

[19] Dickinson, *Supplementary Report* (13 January 1978), Records No. 2342.

McCullough told the press.[20] It was a keystone in plans to revitalize Rockford's struggling downtown.

In room 425 at the Downtown Ramada Inn in Milwaukee, Wisconsin, Ann Nelson reached a final decision to divorce her husband of thirteen years. She had called Ernie Johnson from the hotel room the previous afternoon, and asked him to stop by so they could talk about the situation. While he was in the room, a courier delivered a bouquet of autumn flowers from Ann's husband, Simon Peter Nelson. Ernie came back for an hour later that night, then went home. He called Ann again Friday morning to see how she felt, but her mood had not changed.[21]

Back in Rockford, Karl Winkler and a friend met Simon Peter Nelson at the YMCA, which overlooked the Rock River just northeast of the Whitman Street Bridge. It was the first time Winkler had seen Nelson since he cut his hair and shaved his beard, so he hardly recognized him. The three ran around the track and Nelson, weighing nearly 300 pounds, could barely keep up. According to Winkler, Nelson "seemed to be in a good state of mind," but he left right after the run. Winkler ate a sandwich, said goodbye to his other friend, and then headed back to his office. There he received a message to call Ann Nelson at the hotel in Milwaukee, but was unable to do so until about 3:00pm. She had made up her mind once and for all, she told him. She wanted Winkler, her friend and attorney, to draw up the divorce papers. "Would you like me to tell Pete, or do you want to wait until you come back on Saturday to tell him yourself?" he asked. Not only did Ann want Winkler to make the call, but she also wanted him to meet her at the bus station when she returned to Rockford. She was afraid of what her husband might do.[22]

Nelson had threatened suicide before, once after his first wife left him, and again after being married to Ann for about ten

---

[20] "State OKs Metro Centre," *Morning Star* (Rockford) 6 January 1978.

[21] F. Speracino and Det. C. Jackson, *Statement of Ernie Lee Johnson, Case #943-263* (Rockford Police Dept., 11 January 1978), Records No. 1777-1778.

[22] R. Gloe and Sgt. Galvanoni, *Supplementary Report, Case #943-263* (Rockford Police Dept., 13 January 1978), Records No. 2334.

years. In 1974, a family friend had taken Ann out to a bar after dinner. Nelson found them, and in his words, "something clicked." He slapped her and made a scene, after which he checked into a motel room and planned to commit suicide. Later, he held a shotgun to his chest and asked Ann to pull the trigger. "You're killing me," he told her. "You might as well go ahead and kill me all the way."[23] There was also a history of suicide in his family. In 1955, Nelson's father committed suicide on his wife's birthday, when Nelson was around 22-years-old. He later found notes written by his father that blamed his family for not caring about him.[24]

On the ninth floor of the Talcott Building in the office of Management Recruiters, Inc., Nelson worked diligently at his desk. He had all but stopped socializing with his coworkers in order to focus on his clients. The phone rang. It was Karl Winkler. "I'm busy," Nelson said. "Is this important?"

"Yes," Winkler replied.

"Is it about Ann?"

"Yes."

Winkler told his friend that Ann had made a decision, and the two agreed to meet at Jack's or Better, a restaurant and lounge formerly located at 327 West Jefferson Street, in an hour.[25] Nelson abandoned his work and rushed out the door, stopping only to throw on his coat and mention to Cynthia, the office secretary and bookkeeper, that he had to leave for personal reasons. He was visibly upset and said he would call later to explain.[26]

After school let out for the day, Andy, Nelson's 8-year-old son, walked over to Marie Kant's home to pick up his two youngest siblings, David and Rose Ann (Rosie). Marie had frequently babysat David and Rosie since the Nelsons moved to Rockford. Andy mentioned that the three kids were going to go home and build a

---

[23] Carl H. Hamann, M.D., to Judge John S. Ghent, 16 May 1978.
[24] Register-Star (Rockford) 20 May 1978.
[25] Gloe and Galvanoni, Records No. 2335.
[26] Dickinson, Statement of Michael Weldon, Records No. 314.

snowman, and that their mother was gone for the weekend.[27] Rosie, 5, then went over to the home of Cynthia Auston, who let the young girl play with her daughter and sometimes spend the night. On that particular day, Rosie seemed "unusually quiet" and left for home at about 4:30 in the afternoon, as the sun was setting.[28]

The temperature was retreating from a high of 35 degrees and light snow flurries trickled down from the overcast sky when Nelson met Winkler in the parking lot of Jack's or Better. The two went in together and sat in a booth for some privacy. Nelson ordered a lite beer, and Winkler ordered a martini. Winkler, an average looking man sporting large, thick glasses and a comb over, gave his friend the bad news that Ann had decided to go ahead with the divorce. He later told investigators, "Pete did not show much emotion and acted cool, and looked like he was ready to accept it and make the best of it."[29] Winkler mentioned that Ann wanted Nelson to move out of their house, and he agreed that would be for the best.[30]

At a little before 5pm, Doug Hamm, a commercial photographer from Fontana, Wisconsin, entered Jack's or Better and noticed Nelson and Winkler talking and having drinks. He pulled up a seat at the bar and ordered a cocktail. Hamm was acquainted with Nelson through membership in a service club in Beloit, but the two had never been close friends. Shortly thereafter, Winkler stood up to leave and Nelson went to use the phone. He called Michael Weldon at the office and briefly explained what was happening. He asked for some time off from work and an advance on his regular check. Weldon agreed. Nelson also said he was going to try and work things out with his wife, but that he might have to stay somewhere for several days. Weldon suggested that he stay with Mike Clark, a coworker, friend, and frequent drinking buddy.

---

[27] Kris Dickinson #82, *Supplementary Report, Case #943-263* (Rockford Police Dept., 7 January 1978), Records No. 307-308.

[28] Det. R. Bast #163, *Supplementary Report, Case #943-263* (Rockford Police Dept., 7 January 1978), Records No. 274.

[29] Gloe and Galvanoni, Records No. 2335.

[30] Donnelli and Otwell, Records No. 425.

Nelson then said he would pick up his check at Mike and Dale's Lounge later that evening.[31] The two said their goodbyes, and Nelson joined Doug Hamm at the bar.

Nelson told Hamm about the divorce, and asked him if he would watch the kids while he took some clothes over to a friend's house. Hamm agreed, but not being an inquisitive person, he didn't ask for any details. At about 6pm, Nelson said, "I have to go over to the Lafayette to pick up a check," and then left. He would return a short time later.[32]

Meanwhile, Michael Weldon had gone to Mike and Dale's Lounge, left the check with his bartender, Wayne, and then went downstairs to talk with his manager. A little after 6pm, Nelson entered the lounge and spoke with Wayne, who handed him the check. He ordered a beer, but only took a few sips before he told the bartender he would call Weldon later that night and headed out the door. Later, Wayne mentioned to Dale Dyer, co-owner of Mike and Dale's Lounge, that Nelson seemed depressed.[33]

Nelson then walked a block north up Church Street to Jack's or Better, at the northeast corner of Church and Jefferson, where Doug Hamm was waiting. "Mike was busy," Nelson told him. "I'll just talk to him later." He declined to order a drink, then said, "I'm going home. Meet me there between 7:30 and 8:00pm."

"Fine, see you then," Hamm agreed.[34]

In the meantime, Karl Winkler called Ann Nelson at the hotel in Milwaukee to let her know how her husband reacted to news of the divorce. He told her that Nelson had taken it well and that everything would be all right. "Pete will meet you at the bus station in Rockford Saturday afternoon at 4:10pm," he said. "Everything is going to be all right."[35] The line between client and friend was particularly blurry, and he felt compelled to guide both

---

[31] Dickinson, *Statement of Michael Weldon,* Records No. 314.

[32] Kris Dickinson #82 and Charles Bishop, *Statement of Douglas D. Hamm, Case #943-263* (Rockford Police Dept., 11 January 1978), Records No. 354.

[33] Dickinson, *Supplementary Report* (7 January 1978), Records No. 307.

[34] Dickinson and Bishop, *Statement of Douglas D. Hamm,* Records No. 354.

[35] Gloe and Galvanoni, Records No. 2335.

Ann and her husband through the situation as painlessly as possible. He was convinced that with the children at home, Nelson would not do anything foolish.

At around 7pm, Bobby Andrew knocked on the door of 1425 Camp Avenue. Bobby, 13, was a paperboy for the Rockford *Morning Star*, and as usual on Friday evening, he was making his rounds to collect the delivery fee. Jennifer Nelson answered the door, and he told her he was there to collect. She left the door open while she went to fetch her father, but the boy stayed on the porch. From this vantage point, he saw Simon Peter Nelson walk into a room with Jennifer, and then Jennifer came back with a check for $3.10. Bobby put their payment in his pocket and left for the next house.[36] That was the last time he would see any of the Nelson children.

Shortly thereafter, Doug Hamm arrived at the house with a pizza and a six-pack of beer. He later told investigators that Nelson was being "very nice with the kids." He handed his children passes to the YMCA and made sure they signed them and put them in a place where they would not be lost.[37] A short time later, Karl Winkler arrived at the house and let himself in. He had tried to call several times after 8pm, but the line was dead. The operator told him something was wrong with the Nelsons' phone. Concerned, he rushed over to 1425 Camp Ave., and was relieved when Jennifer Nelson greeted him at the door. Pretzel, the family's brown dachshund, trailed obediently at her heels. He found Doug Hamm and Simon Peter Nelson in the kitchen. He sat down, and Nelson's daughter Rosie climbed onto his lap. "I tried to call several times," he said, "but your phone wasn't working."

Nelson offered him a beer, then got up to check all the phones in the house. He found the upstairs phone was off the hook, so he put the handset on the receiver and came back downstairs. According to Doug Hamm, Winkler said he was supposed to call Ann about the plan for Nelson to pick her up at the bus station the next day. Nelson was getting ready to move some clothes over to

---

[36] Robert Combs, *Statement of Bobby Andrew, Case #943-263* (Rockford Police Dept., 8 January 1978), Records No. 409.

[37] Dickinson and Bishop, *Statement of Douglas D. Hamm,* Records No. 354.

his friend's house, so Winkler said he would call later to go over the plan for Saturday one more time. He left soon after, and called Ann when he got home to let her know everything was all right.[38] He then settled in to watch *Up the Down Staircase* (1967), a film about a young, idealistic English teacher in a New York City public high school, "to come down from telling a good friend his marriage was bad."[39]

Nelson packed several shirts and pairs of pants and other personal items into a suitcase and a large briefcase and carried them out to his station wagon. When they saw this, Simon, Jr. and Andrew, the two oldest boys, became visibly upset. Nelson tried to assure them his absence would only be temporary.[40] He left Hamm with his children and drove to Mike Clark's home to drop off his clothes.

Back at home, Jennifer Nelson was putting her siblings to bed. She led her four brothers, Matthew, David, Andrew, and Simon, Jr. to the bedroom on the third floor. The third floor of the house was a finished attic with one large room and three mattresses on the floor. Two closets and a furnace room were on the north side of the attic, and a third closet was inside the large room at the top of the stairs. Two mattresses were positioned perpendicular to the west wall, and one rested parallel to the east wall. Matthew and David lay down together on the mattress near the west wall closest to the stairs. David was wearing a dark blue pullover shirt and a diaper. They shared a quilt patterned with blue flowers and a gray and blue U.S. Navy blanket to keep out the cold. Andrew, who was wearing a green pullover shirt and black corduroy pants, lay on the mattress closest to them. Simon, Jr. settled down on the mattress on the other side of the room, covering himself with a red sleeping bag and thin blue sheet. He wore a green and black striped shirt

---

[38] Gloe and Galvanoni, Records No. 2335; Dickinson and Bishop, *Statement of Douglas D. Hamm*, Records No. 354-355.

[39] "Not guilty plea likely for Nelson," *Morning Star* (Rockford) 11 January 1978.

[40] "Nelson recalls murder night," *Register-Star* (Rockford) 21 May 1978.

and black pants.[41] Finally, Jennifer led Rose Ann to the northwest bedroom on the second floor, to the left of the stairs. She wrapped her sister in a pink housecoat and tucked her into a brown and purple blanket on a large king sized bed. The phone that had been off the hook earlier in the evening sat on a small table on the north side of the bed. Another table was on the opposite side of the bed, near the door. Both were littered with empty beer cans and ash trays filled with cigarette butts.[42] She said goodnight and headed downstairs, where Doug Hamm was watching television and dozing in a small room at the back of the house.

At about 9:30pm, the phone rang. It was Karl Winkler. Groggy, Hamm took a message that Nelson should meet his wife at the bus station Saturday afternoon. He hung up and lay back down on the couch, but hardly closed his eyes again when the phone rang a second time. It was Nelson, calling from Mike Clark's house. Hamm related Winkler's message, and Nelson said he would call him. "Don't bother," Hamm said. "He just wanted to let you know where to meet Ann."

"I'm going to call him anyway," Nelson said. "I want to make sure Ann is fine."

Hamm hung up and closed his eyes again. The next time he opened them, he was aware that Nelson had come home. He heard voices in the kitchen over the soft chatter of the television. It was Nelson and Jennifer, talking about the divorce. "Everything is going to be all right," Nelson said. "Mommy and I are going to work things out. Don't worry. Mommy says I have to move out of the house, but it doesn't mean I don't love you. You just have to be a big, strong girl like you've always been. I won't be far away." They hugged each other and cried for a few moments.[43] Hamm dozed off.

---

[41] Det. Rinehart, *Supplementary Report, Case #943-263* (Rockford Police Dept., 7 January 1978), Records No. 335-338.

[42] Det. Forsyth, *Supplementary Report, Case #943-263* (Rockford Police Dept., 7 January 1978), Records No. 367-369.

[43] Dickinson and Bishop, *Statement of Douglas D. Hamm*, Records No. 355; *Register-Star* (Rockford) 21 May 1978.

Exhausted from the day's events, Jennifer ascended the stairs to the second floor bedroom where Rose Ann was sound asleep. She changed into a blue t-shirt, grabbed her two favorite stuffed animals, a frog and cat, and settled into a red sleeping bag near the edge of the bed. She lay on her side, facing the doorway, and closed her eyes.[44]

Downstairs, her father sat by the phone and began to make a series of calls. First he called a client, who had gone to a job interview that afternoon, to check on his or her progress. Then, at around 11:00pm, he called Michael Weldon to "give him the full scoop" about what was happening between him and Ann. He told his boss that they had been having problems lately, and that Ann had laid down some ground rules if he wanted to save their marriage. He was trying to live within those rules and had cut his hair, shaved, and started a workout routine to show how committed he was. "I want to do the best I can to get the point across to her I'm really trying to meet things she wants," he said. He was not sure how things would work out, but in case they did not, he dropped off clothes with Mike Clark so he could stay with him. "I really appreciate the opportunity you gave me," he said. "I won't let you down, but I might have to leave work abruptly if I have to see Ann. Things might be sticky for a while. I really wish I could tell you this in person. The most important thing to me right now is my wife and kids."[45]

The whole conversation lasted nearly 30 minutes. Weldon later told investigators, "There was a total indication that he was getting this thing resolved."[46]

Next, Nelson called Ernie Johnson, who was asleep at his home in Waukesha, Wisconsin, about 15 miles west of Milwaukee. The braying of the phone woke him, and when he looked at the clock, the time was 11:41pm. Nelson sounded desperate. He told Johnson that Ann was at the Ramada Inn in Milwaukee and that she wanted a divorce, unaware that Johnson had spoken with her at

---

[44] Forsyth, Records No. 367-368.

[45] "Slayings followed separation," *Morning Star* (Rockford) 9 January 1978.

[46] Dickinson, *Statement of Michael Weldon,* Records No. 315.

the hotel earlier that day. Nelson pleaded with him to go there as soon as possible and talk Ann out of it. "Do you want me to go tonight, or tomorrow morning?" Johnson asked.

"Can you go right away?" Nelson replied. "And call me after you talk to her."

Johnson agreed to go, but did not leave until nearly an hour later.[47] As Johnson prepared to go to Milwaukee, Nelson called his mother-in-law, Rosemary Wilmeth, in Indianapolis.

According to Mrs. Wilmeth, the two simply discussed basic facts about the separation and pending divorce. She was tight-lipped with investigators, and did not reveal any specifics about their conversation.[48] According to Nelson, his mother-in-law berated and insulted him. She called him a "failure" and a "bum" and blamed him for the failure of the marriage.[49] Shortly after he hung up the phone, Mrs. Wilmeth rang her daughter at the hotel in Milwaukee and told her Nelson had called. If they talked about anything else, it is unknown.

Ernie Johnson left his house in Waukesha around 12:30am and arrived at the Downtown Ramada Inn in Milwaukee around 1:00am. He went straight to the lobby. Mark Malecki and Alan Januszewski were working the night shift as desk clerks at the hotel. Johnson approached Januszewski and asked where he might buy some beer. After directing him to a nearby store, Johnson left and returned a short time later carrying "what appeared to be two six-packs in a brown bag."[50]

For the fourth time in two days, Johnson was back in Room 425 with Ann. "Pete called me tonight and asked me to come up and try to talk you out of the divorce," he said.

"He must be calling everyone," Ann replied.

---

47 Speracino and Jackson, *Statement of Ernie Lee Johnson*, Records No. 1778.

48 Kris Dickinson #82 and R. Bast, *Supplementary Report, Case #943-263* (Rockford Police Dept., 11 January 1978), Records No. 1809.

49 "Nelson found guilty," *Morning Star* (Rockford) 23 May 1978.

50 Det. C. Jackson and F. Speracino, *Supplementary Report, Case #943-263* (Rockford Police Dept., 9 January 1978), Records No. 450.

No sooner had she said that, Nelson called the hotel room. Ann and he spoke briefly and went over the plans for later that afternoon. Ann was supposed to take a Greyhound bus from Milwaukee at 1:10pm and arrive in Rockford at 4:10pm, where Nelson would pick her up. She said her soon-to-be ex-husband sounded almost sheepish, since their attorney, Karl Winkler, told him not to call her in Milwaukee anymore.

About 45 minutes later, around 2:15am, Nelson called again. This time, his demeanor had changed and he sounded like he had been drinking. While Ann and he talked, Johnson tried not to listen, but he overheard bits and pieces. Nelson could not understand why Ann was leaving him. He asked her about the children, and told her that he wanted custody of them. "It'll be up to a judge to decide," she replied. "I don't want you to call me anymore," she added, irritated. "You can pick me up at the bus station, take me home, and leave. Don't call me again; not at home, not at work. I don't love you anymore. It's over. It just won't work."[51] Later, Nelson testified that Ann had said, "I'm keeping the children. I don't love you anymore. I don't ever want to see you again. I don't want you calling or bothering me again."

"Honey, don't say that," he replied. This was the last time he called the motel room in Milwaukee. According to Nelson, after he hung up the phone, "I died. Everything fell apart in pieces on the floor." He looked for a gun in the family room, but was unable to find one, so he went out to the garage.[52]

Doug Hamm, who was still sleeping in the Nelsons' TV room, woke up. Someone had turned off the television. There were lights on in the kitchen and living room, but the whole house was quiet. A single log burned in the fireplace in the front room, but Hamm did not remember a fire there before he dozed off. *Everyone must be sleeping*, he probably thought. He crept out of the house

---

[51] Dickinson, *Supplementary Report* (13 January 1978), 1; Speracino and Jackson, *Statement of Ernie Lee Johnson,* Records No. 1778.

[52] *Register-Star* (Rockford) 21 May 1978.

and into the frosty night, passing Nelson's station wagon on the street as he headed to his car.[53]

At the home of Ann and Peter Boline, who lived across the alley from the Nelsons, their German shepherd was acting strangely. The dog came into their bedroom shivering and whimpering. Ann Boline, wrapped tightly in a thick robe, let him outside and noticed there was a light on in the Nelson's kitchen. Boline later told police that her dog had never behaved that way before.[54]

The house at 1425 Camp Avenue was quiet, but in Simon Peter Nelson's mind, he raged. He returned from the garage with a large rubber mallet and antler-handled hunting knife. He found the first floor empty, so he crept up a flight of stairs to the second floor. He peered into the northwest bedroom, where he saw his two daughters sleeping soundly on the king sized bed, then proceeded to the bathroom at the other end of the hall and removed his shirt. He threw that on the floor, leaving himself dressed in a plain white t-shirt. He returned to the northwest bedroom and gently pushed the door open. A faint beam of light fell on the sleeping girls. Their brown dachshund, pretzel, was curled up in the blankets between them. It was the bed where his wife and he used to sleep.

Acting quickly, Nelson opened pretzel's throat with his hunting knife. Blood sprayed, and the little dog convulsed briefly and stretched out on its back. The girls stirred but did not wake. Assurances that "things will be all right" disappeared with the sickening smack of a black rubber mallet against the side of Jennifer's head. A knife slash to the throat followed the blow. More blood. He killed Rose Ann in the same way—knocking her unconscious with the mallet, then cutting her throat. His white t-shirt was painted with a spatter of crimson.

Blood pooled on the floor beside the bed as Nelson turned and walked toward the northeast bedroom as if in a trance. The

---

[53] Dickinson and Bishop, *Statement of Douglas D. Hamm*, Records No. 355.

[54] J. Morse #14, *Supplementary Report, Case #943-263* (Rockford Police Dept., 7 January 1978), Records No. 299.

room was empty aside from three chest of drawers, a corner cabinet, and a box filled with old clothes. The stairs to the third floor were right behind the door in the darkened room. It was thirteen steps to the top.

Snowflakes danced outside the attic window, illuminated by the moon. The four children asleep in the room were, perhaps, dreaming of aliens from outer space. Earlier that week, their father had left work early to take them to see the movie *Close Encounters of the Third Kind*. Now he stood in the doorway, mallet in one hand, knife in the other. If he hesitated at all, asked himself what he was doing, or had second thoughts, there is no evidence of it. His children would never dream again. He struck Matthew on the right side of his head "with such force that the side of his head was caved in and his skull was shattered." He did the same to 3-year-old David, with such violence that his shoulders and head were pushed off the mattress. The boy was unmistakably dead, but Nelson stabbed him in the stomach anyway before moving on to the adjacent mattress, where Andrew lay. He was lying face down. Nelson struck him on the left side of the head with the mallet and then cut his throat with the knife. Finally, he crossed to the other side of the room. Simon, Jr. lay on a mattress parallel to the wall. Nelson struck him in the right side of the head and then stabbed him several times in and around his neck. He grabbed his son's arms and attempted to pull him off the mattress, but abandoned the effort after a short time.[55]

Nelson's chest heaved. He was surrounded by gore. In the words of Detective Rinehart, "Blood was spattered on the walls, ceiling, and floor of the room. There was not any area of the room of any size that did not have some evidence of the victims on it."[56] Nelson crossed the room to the closet near the top of the stairs and dropped the heavy mallet on the floor next to a discarded pillow. He then descended the stairs to the second floor and peeled off his blood soaked undershirt. After stuffing it in a brown paper bag, he deposited the bag next to a table in the southeast bedroom. The

[55] Rinehart, *Supplementary Report*, Records No. 336.
[56] Ibid.

lives of his children extinguished, he removed the rest of his clothes and stepped in the shower.

The phone rang.

A Shocking Confession, a Grisly Discovery

Back at the Ramada Inn in Milwaukee, Ann Nelson was frantically calling home. She gave up after nearly a dozen attempts, and called Karl Winkler. There was no answer. Finally, at about 4:30am Saturday morning, Ann called the Rockford Police Department to perform a welfare check. According to Ernie Johnson, the operator told Ann they would check, but could not call her back. 30 minutes later, she called the Rockford PD again and was told that officers had been dispatched, but that there was no response at the house.

Around the same time, 13-year-old Bobby Andrew pedaled down Camp Avenue on his bicycle, delivering the morning newspaper. He noticed Nelson's "old, beat up station wagon" pulling away from the curb in front of the Nelsons' home. He noticed it because there was usually no traffic on the street that early. As usual, Bobby tossed the newspaper on the Nelsons' driveway and continued down the street.[57]

At 5:42am, Officers Dahm and Beauflis were dispatched to Camp Avenue to deliver a telephone number to Simon Peter Nelson where he could reach Ann, and to ask him to call as soon as possible. When the two officers arrived, they saw lights on in an upstairs room and in the dining room. They knocked on the door for several minutes and looked into the windows, but did not receive any answer or notice anything out of the ordinary.[58] They knocked loudly enough to wake John Bates, who was asleep next door. He did not get up to investigate the noise, however, because he assumed it was Nelson coming home after a long night of drinking.

---

[57] *Register-Star* (Rockford) 8 January 1978.
[58] T. Dahm and Beauflis, *General Case Report, Case #943-297* (Rockford Police Dept., 7 January 1978), Records No. 304.

It was 91 miles from Nelson's doorstep to the Downtown Ramada Inn in Milwaukee, Wisconsin. Nelson probably took the most direct route: N. 2nd Street to Interstate 90 from South Beloit, to WIS 15, to I-894 and I-94 in Milwaukee. WIS 15 had been completed two years earlier. Its name was later changed to Interstate 43, which readers are familiar with today. The journey took about 1 hour and 40 minutes of driving through the cold, dark night with only the headlights of Nelson's 1970 Pontiac Catalina Station Wagon to light the way.

Working diligently behind the front desk at the Ramada Inn in Milwaukee, Mark Malecki thought he saw Nelson in the lobby by the drinking fountain and the elevators around 5:45am. Ernie Johnson, however, told investigators that Nelson knocked on the door of Ann's hotel room at around 6:30am. This means he must have left Rockford sometime between 4:00 and 4:45am, around the time the paperboy saw Nelson's vehicle pull away from the curb in front of his house.

When Johnson opened the hotel room door and saw Nelson standing on the other side, he hardly recognized his friend without his long hair and beard. He told investigators that Nelson "kind of smiled." Also, "His eyes were kind of glassy like he had been drinking." Nelson did not answer a barrage of questions from either Ernie Johnson or Ann. Instead, he put his arm around Ann and asked for a last kiss goodbye. He then told them to call a priest. "Call two priests and call the police," he purportedly said. Ann repeatedly asked him about their children, which made Nelson upset.

"Forget it for a minute," Johnson said, and told Ann to sit down. She did. Johnson began to look up churches in the phone book and called several, with no result. "I'm not Catholic," he said. "I don't know what to say." Ann told her husband to take the phone, but he did not get a response either. At that point, Nelson got up and went into the bathroom. Ann told Johnson to go to the lobby and call the police. He hesitated, not wanting to leave her alone with her husband, but she insisted.[59]

After Johnson left the room, Nelson came out of the bathroom and Ann again asked him about the children. "They're dead," he allegedly replied. "They are all dead. How do you feel about that?" He blamed the divorce for his actions, and told Ann she would have to live with the guilt. That was her punishment.

In court, she described what happened next. "I stared at him. He kept repeating it over and over. 'They're all dead. There is no way you or anyone else can get to them in time. You and your damn skating matter more than me. So I killed the kids, and I did it in such a spectacular way you will never be able to work again. That way, you will have lost the kids and your job and will have nothing.'"[60]

Panicked, Ann fled the room and tried to get the elevator, but Nelson was faster. He maneuvered between her and the elevator and ushered her back to the room. "I wanted to see the look on your face when I told you," he said. According to Ann, he then said he was going to kill himself by running his car into the biggest object he could find.

"I asked him to leave and went over and opened the door," Ann told investigators. "He came over and hit me in the face. He then punched me in the stomach and I went down. I tried to crawl over to the bathroom and he kept kicking me and kicking me. I screamed and tried to crawl under the counter in the bathroom."[61] Ann later told friends that Nelson has started to beat her because "she hadn't given her husband the reaction he wanted to see, and he became enraged when she didn't react."[62]

Meanwhile, in the hotel lobby, Johnson asked desk clerks Malecki and Januszewski to call the police because there was

---

[59] Speracino and Jackson, *Statement of Ernie Lee Johnson,* Records No. 1779.

[60] "Ann Nelson: He kept repeating it, they're all dead," *Morning Star* (Rockford) 19 May 1978.

[61] F. Speracino and Det. C. Jackson, *Statement of Anne Wilmeth Nelson, Case #943-263* (Rockford Police Dept., 7 January 1978), Records No. 2342.

[62] Dickinson and Bast, Records No. 444.

trouble in Room 425. The clerk was so shocked that he couldn't complete the call, so Johnson took the phone from him and spoke with the Milwaukee police. "Send a car in a hurry," he said. Just a few minutes later, two officers from the Milwaukee Police Department arrived and accompanied Johnson back to the fourth floor. They were just in time to hear Ann scream. The policemen rushed into the room and pulled Nelson off his wife and handcuffed him. Johnson later described Ann's injuries. "I saw that her lip was cut and her cheek was bruised and she also had a cut on the back of her head that was bleeding. She also had a cut on her left ear and had blood on her arm."

"I'm sorry," Nelson said as the police officers removed him from the room.[63] They took his glasses, which were spattered with blood, as evidence. During Nelson's arrest, his demeanor changed. When the officers asked why he was attacking his wife, he replied that she had merely fallen and he was helping her up. When they asked about his children, he said they were safe at home with Jennifer, his oldest, to look after them.[64]

At 7:18am, Officer Carnal of the Milwaukee Police Department called the Winnebago County Sheriff's Department from the Ramada Inn and requested a welfare check on behalf of Ann Nelson. The Sheriff's Department relayed the message to Rockford PD. At 7:41am, Communications Dispatcher Robert Bauer sent Patrol Officer Stephen Pirages to 1425 Camp Avenue. Pirages, 24, had been a patrolman with the Rockford Police Department for two and a half years. The sun was peaking over the horizon when he arrived. He did not see anything out of the ordinary, although the dining room light was still on. Then, at 8:10am, Ann called the Rockford Police Department and told the operator that her husband had confessed to murdering their children, and that she gave them permission to break into the house if necessary.

---

[63] Speracino and Jackson, *Statement of Ernie Lee Johnson,* Records No. 1780.

[64] Dickinson and Bast, Records No. 444.

Patrolman Pirages and Sergeant Gordon Mayer quickly returned to the scene.[65]

Officers Colin Anderson and Don Smith followed in a white car, which was used as a makeshift ambulance. They were soon joined by Larry Michealson, who was running radar in the 700 block of N. Main Street. When Pirages and Mayer arrived, Pirages knocked on the door of 1427 Camp Ave. and asked neighbor John Bates for an extension ladder. Bates obliged, and Officer Pirages took it to the back of the Nelson home, where there was a screened in porch on the second floor. He climbed up to the window and tried to open it, or at least look inside. It was no use. The windows were locked and the drapes drawn, although he could tell there was a light on in the adjacent room. Lieutenant Jacob Gessner, a Patrol Bureau shift commander who was on route to the scene, advised the officers that they should forcibly enter, since all other available means of entry had been exhausted.[66] Officer Michealson obtained a screw driver from his tool kit. With Officer Smith's help, he first pried off the storm window and then forced open the primary window. According to Smith, he entered the house first, followed by Michealson, Anderson, and Sgt. Mayer.[67] Officer Pirages also entered the home, but there are contradictory statements regarding the exact moment.

The first floor was silent and empty, with ashes smoldering in the fireplace. The officers marched up the creaking stairs to the second floor and split up to check its five rooms. Smith went straight to the master bedroom, which was located at the northwest corner of the house. As soon as he flicked on the light, his eyes fell on a sickening and gruesome scene. Officer Pirages, speaking for all

---

[65] James M. Cram, *Report to Chief* (Winnebago County Sheriff's Department), Records No. 281; Robert Bauer, *Officer's Report - Report to Chief* (Rockford Police Dept., 7 January 1978), Records No. 286; S. Pirages #245, *Supplementary Report, Case #943-263* (Rockford Police Dept., 7 January 1978).

[66] S. Pirages, *Crime Against Person Case Report, Case #943-263* (Rockford Police Dept., 7 January 1978), Records No. 259.

[67] D. Smith, *Supplementary Report, Case #943-263* (Rockford Police Dept., 7 January 1978), Records No. 265; Michealson, *Supplementary Report, Case #943-263* (Rockford Police Dept., 7 January 1978), Records No. 276.

present, later told the *Register Star* how it felt seeing the Nelson children for the first time. "It's hard to describe... shock... and sort of a feeling of helplessness, I guess." He added, "Probably your gut reaction would be to vomit, but you've got to do what you've got to do."[68]

At exactly 8:31am, the officers went back downstairs and Smith radioed Sgt. Peterson to tell him what they found. Peterson informed him that there were six children, not two, so Smith, Pirages, Mayer, Anderson, and Michealson climbed the stairs to the attic. An equally gruesome sight greeted them there. They secured the crime scene and waited for backup. Chief Deputy Coroner Ruth Anderson arrived at about 9am, followed shortly by Winnebago County Coroner Dr. P. John Seward, to confirm the identities of the victims and oversee removal of their bodies. Police Chief Delbert Peterson and even Rockford Mayor Robert McGaw soon joined them at the scene. Camp Avenue, usually a quiet street, was flooded with onlookers and the press. Lt. Gessner told the *Register Star*, "[It was] a real massacre, the worst I've ever seen... It's probably the worst you'll see anyplace."[69] Later, Chief Deputy Coroner Anderson said, "In all the cases I've been on, this was the only one where I came out of there shaking. They were such beautiful children."[70]

Back in Milwaukee, Ernie Johnson was on the phone with Karl Winkler. Ann had made the call from her hotel room, but was too shaken up to speak with him. It was then that both Johnson and Winkler learned about the fate of Ann's children for the first time. Hearing the alarming news, Winkler told her he would come to Milwaukee right away. Johnson left to pick up his wife, then when he returned, they followed Milwaukee Detective Zuehlke and a policewoman as they took Ann to the police station.[71]

---

[68] "Routine call turns into nightmare," *Register-Star* (Rockford) 8 January 1978.

[69] "Six children found slain; father charged," *Register-Star* (Rockford) 7 January 1978.

[70] "Simon Peter Nelson held without bond," *Register-Star* (Rockford) 8 January 1978.

[71] Speracino and Jackson, *Statement of Ernie Lee Johnson,* Records No. 1780.

Around 9:30am, Rockford Detectives F. Speracino and C. Jackson were called into work and asked to drive to Milwaukee, Wisconsin to extradite Simon Peter Nelson and bring him back to Rockford. Winnebago County Assistant State's Attorney Robert Gemignani accompanied them. When they arrived, they took a statement from Ann Nelson, then attended Nelson's extradition hearing before Judge Christ Seraphim. The hearing was held in a small room in Milwaukee PD headquarters. Judge Seraphim allowed cameras and other recording equipment into the hearing for the first time since Wisconsin imposed a ban on recording devices during court proceedings in the 1960s. "I am going to permit you to come in," he told the press, "but you are going to have to behave yourselves. I don't want flash bulbs all over the place."[72] Nelson, whose glasses were still in an evidence bag, had to have the waiver of extradition read to him. Tears trickled down his face as he listened to the Judge, and he signed the waivers.

Later, Thomas Cannon, director of the Legal Aid Society of Milwaukee, alleged that Nelson's extradition was improper. Among more minor omissions, Judge Seraphim had apparently forgotten to inform Nelson that Illinois had the death penalty until after he signed the extradition waivers. A transcript of the hearing shows Judge Seraphim saying, "Oh! I neglected to say one other thing... Do you understand that in the State of Illinois, murder is punishable by death?" Nelson was not aware of that, he replied, but it was too late to revoke his signature.[73]

Outside, Karl Winkler wrapped Ann in a heavy fur coat and escorted her to his car through a mob of questioning reporters and flashing cameras. Inside the police station, Detectives Speracino and Jackson read Nelson his rights and asked him if he was willing to talk. He was, but he claimed that he could not remember the events of that evening. He broke down in tears, and asked for a lawyer. At around 5:15pm, they left for Rockford. Nelson slept nearly the whole way back.

---

[72] "Court allows cameras at hearing," *Register-Star* (Rockford) 8 January 1978.
[73] "Simon Nelson extradition questioned," *Register-Star* (Rockford) 28 January 1978.

Epilogue

A dozen mourners stood in solemn silence in Rockford's Calvary Cemetery as five hearses slowly pulled up to the empty burial sites. One by one, in temperatures of 10 degrees below zero, pallbearers removed six small, white coffins and readied them for burial. There were no flowers. Ann Nelson was not present. She had attended a private funeral with close friends and relatives on Monday. A public mass for the six Nelson children, Jennifer, Simon Jr., Andrew, Matthew, Rose Ann, and David, was held at St. Peter's Cathedral that afternoon. An hour before the burial, on Wednesday, January 11, Simon Peter Nelson pled not guilty to the charges of murder at his arraignment before Winnebago County Circuit Judge Philip J. Reinhard.[74] Public Defender Craig Peterson had been appointed as Nelson's lawyer, since his own attempts to find legal representation had failed. After his arrest, Nelson spoke briefly over the phone with his friend and attorney Karl Winkler, but Winkler said he "did not want to be involved in Nelson's case." Angry at what his friend had done, he added that he didn't want to even see Nelson because he was afraid of what he would do to him.[75]

Nelson's trial began on Monday, May 15, 1978. Public Defender Craig Peterson argued that Nelson had been temporarily insane at the time he committed the murders. Devastated by his pending divorce, he had imagined himself in the person of his deceased father. In his mind, he had committed suicide in the basement, and saw a vision of his father go upstairs and methodically butcher his children. Dr. Lawrence Freedman, an expert on criminal mentality and legal psychiatry, backed up Nelson's claims and said he was genuinely insane during those early morning hours of January 7th. The prosecution, however, produced two psychiatrists and one psychologist to contradict Freedman's opinion. Dr. James Cavanaugh, Dr. Roger Mick, and Dr. Carl

---

[74] "Nelson pleads innocent in slaying of his children," *Morning Star* (Rockford) 12 January 1978.

[75] K. Dickinson and T. Nimmo, *Supplementary Report, Case #943-263* (Rockford Police Dept., 8 January 1978), Records No. 411.

Hamann had all examined and interviewed Nelson and determined that he was sane when he committed the murders. Nelson, they concluded, had acted out of rage and a consuming desire for revenge against his wife.[76]

Bolstering Winnebago County State's Attorney Daniel Doyle's argument was the strange coincidence that Nelson had been reading *Anatomy of a Murder* weeks before he committed the crime. Just like in the novel, Nelson had tried to argue that he was in a "dissociative state" at the time of the murders, leading the prosecution to speculate that he had planned the murders—along with his defense—in advance. "Is it a coincidence?" Doyle reportedly asked the jury. "I'll leave that up to you. I don't think so."[77]

It took the jury less than one and a half hours to find Simon Peter Nelson guilty, but they deadlocked over whether to impose the death penalty. Peterson, Nelson's court-appointed attorney, argued that it would be better to let Nelson suffer in prison than to execute him. "If electrocuting Simon Peter Nelson could bring back [his children], then do it," he said. "Or would it be more cruel, more punishment to make Simon Peter Nelson think about it every day, month, week and year for as long as he shall live?" State's Attorney Doyle argued that Nelson should be executed to deter future child murders. "In this type of case, if by setting an example, you could save the life of some innocent child someday in the future, would that not justify your actions in imposing it?" he asked. According to sources interviewed by the *Morning Star*, the jury voted 11 to 1 against the death penalty, leaving Judge John Ghent to decide on a prison sentence.[78] At the time, Illinois state law required a minimum 14-year prison term for each count of murder, so the judge had to impose a minimum of 84 years. On June 13, 1978, Judge Ghent sentenced Simon Peter Nelson to not less than 100 years nor

---

[76] "Was Nelson sane? The doctors differed," *Morning Star* (Rockford) 23 May 1978.

[77] "Jury determines verdict in less than 1 1/2 hours," *Morning Star* (Rockford) 23 May 1978.

[78] "Nelson escapes execution," *Morning Star* (Rockford) 24 May 1978.

more than 200 years in the Illinois State Penitentiary for each of the six counts of murder. Unless paroled, Nelson would die in prison.

Since beginning his prison sentence, Simon Peter Nelson, now known as Inmate Number C82127, has appealed his conviction in both state and federal court. He has gone before the Illinois Prisoner Review Board 17 times to try and win freedom, but has always been denied. The latest parole hearing took place on October 27, 2011, and the board voted unanimously to deny parole.[79] The last time Nelson was up for parole, in 2008, board member Craig Findley told the *Register Star*, "Almost alone among inmates in custody, he deserves to die in prison. There are not many I would say that about. But this is a crime that can't be forgiven. He can never be released."[80]

After her husband's conviction, Ann Nelson went through with the divorce and sought a return to private life. Simon Peter Nelson, now 82-years-old, spent several years at Menard Correctional Center, a maximum-security prison outside Chester, Illinois, before being transferred to a medium-security facility, Graham Correctional Center in Hillsboro, Illinois. In 1982, while at Menard, Nelson met and married Jewell Friend, a former dean of academic affairs at Southern Illinois University in Carbondale, who was teaching classes at the prison.[81] She died of stomach cancer in 2005.

Nelson has expressed remorse for the murders, and claims he has found a deep religious conviction, but still maintains he is unable to fully remember the events of that long, dark January night in 1978. "All I remember is being split somehow and my father being present—and again, this is irrational—and my telling him not to go up the stairs," he told the Illinois Prisoner Review Board in

---

[79] "Parole board right with Simon Peter Nelson decision," *Register Star* (Rockford) 28 October 2011.

[80] "Board votes to keep Simon Peter Nelson in prison," *Register Star* (Rockford) 19 June 2008.

[81] "Dad expresses remorse for kids' deaths," *Register Star* (Rockford) 4 May 2004.

2004. "This was after I had imagined that I killed myself."[82] After 35 years, Nelson still maintains his insanity defense.

The massacre of the Nelson children continues to haunt Rockford to the present day, and all involved, although three and a half decades have passed, still remember those events in vivid detail. For Officer Stephen Pirages, now retired from the Rockford Police Department, his feelings on Nelson's conviction remain unwavering, "In my opinion, there is no way he should ever breathe a free breath again."[83] There have been many tragic crimes in Rockford's history, but none as shocking, brutal, and with such a lasting impact as the murder of the Nelson children. Simon Peter Nelson's prison sentence may offer a sense of justice, but no punishment can ever remove the stain of this crime from the community, or resurrect Jennifer, Simon Jr., Andrew, Matthew, Rose Ann, and David, whose lives were extinguished at such a young age. Their murder created a moral debt that can never be repaid.

---

[82] Ibid.

[83] "Dad who killed 6 kids, Simon Peter Nelson, shouldn't be freed, cop says," *Register Star* (Rockford) 30 May 2011.

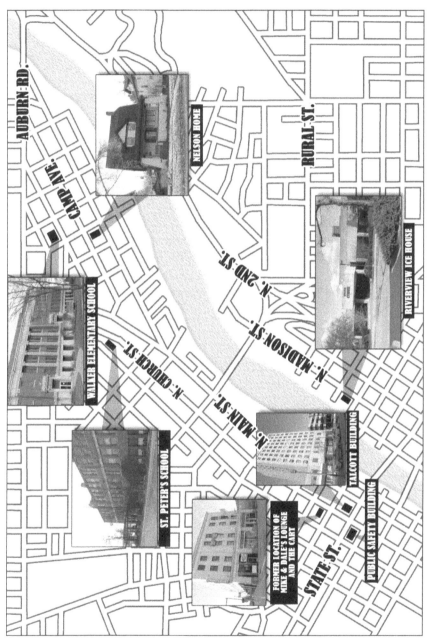

Map of Rockford locations featured in "A Long, Dark Night."

ABOUT THE AUTHORS

HEATH D. ALBERTS is the author of two novels (*Terminal Beginning* & *Last Rights*) as well as one novella (*The Battery Man*), and a marketing and business strategy guide geared toward cottage & small business owners (*Guerrilla Business*). He is a regular contributor to, and co-administrator of, The Rockford Blog (author of the 'Remembrances of Pauline Avenue' & 'Rockford's Own' series'), as well as the co-founder of Digital Ninjas Media, Inc. He is currently at work on his third novel, Photographic Memory, which is scheduled for publication late in 2014. A native of Rockford's west side, and an avid collector of rare & first-edition books, he now resides in Rockton, Illinois with his wife, Wanda, and his malicious cat.

TED BIONDO retired in 2005 after 32 years at Hamilton Sundstrand, including 17 years as an Electrical/Software Engineering Manager. He was a community member of the *Rockford Register Star* Editorial Board and the Community Viewpoint Board in the early 1990s. He has written numerous articles on local, state, and national issues, and was a finalist for the Excalibur Award in 2007.

Ted served three years as vice president of the Rockford School board and just finished his ninth year on the Rock Valley College Board of Trustees, where he served as Board Chair for two years and Finance Committee Chair for seven years. He is currently a member of the Winnebago County board, serves as Chairman of the Finance and Administrative committee, and was appointed to the Budget and Finance subcommittee of the Rockford School Board.

Ted graduated Valedictorian at Central High School (Saint Louis) in 1961, awarded a BSEE degree from Saint Louis University in 1965 and was selected for membership in two national honors fraternities in mathematics and electrical engineering. He and his wife, Patricia, have been married for 49 years, with two children and five grandchildren.

STANLEY CAMPBELL, 53 years old, is a Vietnam veteran and "Rockford's only paid peace activist." He is executive director of

Rockford Urban Ministries, an outreach of the 15 area United Methodist churches (and five others). Mr. Campbell brings 30 years of organizing skills, as well as a good sense of humor and some optimism, to the environmental movement. He was involved in the first time that the Nuclear Regulatory Commission (NRC) denied a license to operate a nuclear reactor.

DAN CREVISTON was born and raised in Rockford. He holds a Bachelor's degree in Business & Commerce and Marketing from Aurora University and currently works as a Comparison Shopping Manager for an Internet marketing agency. He is also the founder and owner of The Rockford Blog, as well as a member of the Rockford Hip Hop Congress. He currently resides in Rockford with his pet dog, Mia.

SCOTT FARRELL is the director of Rockford Operetta Party, and has participated in every major local performing group except for Kantorei. Farrell holds an Associate's Degree from Rock Valley College, and is a member of Phi Mu Alpha Sinfonia. Farrell is also director of Grace Notes at First Presbyterian Church of Winnebago, in addition to his accompanist duties. He has composed twelve light operas, five of which have been performed locally.

ERNIE FUHR grew up on a farm in Rock Island County, Illinois. He moved to Rockford in 1991 to take his first teaching job, and has called it home ever since. He graduated from Western Illinois University with a degree in History/Political Science, and he also holds a Master's in Education Administration from Northern Illinois University. Ernie has an inquisitive mind and a passion for learning and exploring new ideas. He loves researching and writing, and recently authored a biography of Rockford ballplayer Hal Carlson, due to be published in 2014 by SABR (Society for American Baseball Research). Ernie and his wife Stephanie are the proud parents of two tuxedo cats.

JEFF HAVENS is a former staff writer for *The Rock River Times*, a weekly newspaper distributed in northern Illinois. He won a news reporting award from the Illinois Press Association in 2004 for investigative writing about mismanagement at Rock Valley College in Rockford. He also wrote numerous articles about the Mob and public affairs in Rockford. Havens now resides in Helena, Montana, where he is employed and writing a book about the Lewis and Clark expedition.

MICHAEL KLEEN is a Rockford resident with a B.A. in Philosophy and M.A. in History from Eastern Illinois University and a M.S. in Education from Western Illinois University. He owns Black Oak Media, Inc., and has written several books, including *Tales of Coles County, Illinois*; *Legends and Lore of Illinois*; and *Haunting Illinois: A Tourist's Guide to the Weird and Wild Places of the Prairie State*. He is a public speaker on Illinois history and folklore, a freelance columnist, and has presented papers at the Conference on Illinois History in 2007, 2010, and 2011. He was also the Republican candidate for Mayor of Rockford in 2013.

KATHI KRESOL has been researching Rockford's History for the past ten years. She shares the fascinating stories she uncovers through her website at www.hauntedrockford.com and through her tours. Kathi's obsession is history and she loves the opportunity to share this passion through the stories she collects. She gives all the credit for her researching skills to the Rockford Public Library's goddesses of Local History, Jean Lythgoe and Jan Carter.

Kathi has worked at the Rockford Public Library for years. She began teaching history using ghost stories when she homeschooled her children, and wanted to share that experience with the Rockford community. She found the perfect solution in forming Haunted Rockford Paranormal Tours. It has allowed her to work with some great people from all over Illinois and Wisconsin and share the stories of the men, women, and children who settled Rockford and gave so much to create such a rich history.

Kathi's main inspiration comes from her four remarkable children and "the guy who brings her coffee," John. They all support her by allowing her to drag them to historical places, listen to her stories, help her "look for dead guys," and put up with her absences when she disappears to research or write.

D. B. Lane, the pseudonym for Doug Janicke, was born in Freeport, Illinois but has been a longtime Rockford resident. Doug recently received his Associate's degree from Highland Community College in Freeport where he wrote "A Dark Wood" in the spring of 2013 as an assignment for a creative writing course. Currently, he's majoring in English at Rockford University. An accomplished guitarist, Doug has taught music lessons and performed in the Rockford area for many decades. He enjoys writing poetry and prose based in what he refers to as his "neck of the woods," the beautiful northern Illinois corridor stretching from Galena and the Mississippi all the way to Chicago and Lake Michigan.

Doug is fascinated with the periods of American history encompassing his grandparents' immigration, the turn of an exciting century heralding new inventions and promising progress, his parents' struggling childhoods in the midst of economic global meltdown, and the tragedies of two world wars that not only ravaged the planet but also changed humanity and altered the future forever. Doug wants to continue building a body of work including stories, poetry, and novels that expand the characters discovered populating these situations and localities.

Nicole C. Lindsay, a resident of Loves Park for over eight years and a resident of the Rockford area for more than 20 years, has an interest in local history as well as a B.A. in history from Rockford College and a M.A. in Library and Information Studies from the University of Wisconsin-Madison. She is also a member of Phi Alpha Theta, the National History Honor Society. Professionally, she is a freelance writer, editor, and researcher. Her first book, *Images of America: Loves Park* was released in February 2013. She is currently working on her second book.

About the Authors

KAREN MAHIEU LYDDON has lived in Rockford for over 50 years and fondly recalls her years at East High. She is a local history buff and was shocked to discover the East High meteor while reading her husband's uncle's memoirs. For multiple decades, Forrest Lyddon (1899-1982) was the Supervisor of Construction for many buildings in Rockford. He almost kept the Coronado Theater closed on its opening night in 1927 until they fulfilled a safety requirement. Many of his remembrances of Rockford have yet to be revealed. To this day, Karen is the proud reunion co-chair of her E-RAB class of 1969. A large portion of her time is spent communicating with and updating the database for her 720 class members.

JIM PHELPS is a humble shop keep with an import business located on 7th Street called Phoenix Traders. In his past he was an Army SIGINT Intelligence Analyst who wrote reports for national consumers of intelligence like the National Security Agency. He traveled around the Middle East in 1989 with a backpack and camping gear, living in caves and ditches, roof top youth hostels, old crusader fortresses and worked briefly on a Moshav in Israel milking cows before returning to the states to purse a B.B.A. in Marketing from University of Wisconsin in Eau Claire.

A few years later, he earned an A.A.S. in Electromechanical Technology from Chippewa Valley Technical College and worked for a few foreign companies with sales/service offices in the Rockford area where he could use his foreign languages, technical and business skill sets. He daily thanks god for an awful local economy, so he could once again go to work for himself like he did all through his college career and travel again using his language and business skills. If he had it all to do over again, he would prefer to be a surf bum living in his 1982 VW Vanagon Diesel, but, *c'est la vie.*

BRANDON REID has served as assistant editor and senior assistant editor of *The Rock River Times* weekly newspaper in Rockford, Ill., for more than a decade. He is a Rockford native and has a M.S. in journalism from the University of Illinois at Urbana-Champaign and a bachelor's degree in journalism and political science from Drake University. He lives in Machesney Park, Ill., with his wife and two kids.

KEVIN RILOTT lives in Rockford with his wife Donna and two sons. He is a teacher at St. Bernadette School and Director of Religious Education for St. Bernadette Church. Kevin has been involved in pro-life ministry for 20 years and writes for prolifecorner.com.